£2

Baedeker
an Canaria

Baedeker's

GRAN CANARIA

Imprint

91 colour photographs
3 town plans, 1 special plan, 2 general maps, 2 drawings, 2 ground plans, 1 map of communications, 1 map of islands

Text: Birgit Borowski

Editorial work:
Baedeker Stuttgart

English language edition:
Alec Court

Design and layout: Creativ GmbH, Ulrich Kolb, Stuttgart

General direction:
Dr Peter Baumgarten, Baedeker Stuttgart

Cartography:
Franz Kaiser, Sindelfingen; Gert Oberländer, Munich;
Mairs Geographischer Verlag GmbH & Co., Ostfildern-Kemnat (map of islands)

English translation:
James Hogarth

Source of illustrations:
Baedeker-Archiv (1), Borowski (32), Brdel (46), dpa (1), Gugel und Mocha (1), Historia-Photo (2), Linde (1), Museo Arqueológico de Tenerife (4), Museo Diocesano de Arte Sacro (2), Ullstein Bilderdienst (1).

To make it easier to locate the various sights listed in the "A to Z" section of the Guide, their coordinates on the large map of the islands are shown in red at the head of each entry.

Following the tradition established by Karl Baedeker in 1844, sights of particular interest are distinguished by either one or two asterisks.

Only a selection of hotels, restaurants and shops can be given: no reflection is implied, therefore, on establishments not included.

The symbol ⓘ on a town plan indicates the local tourist office from which further information can be obtained. The post-horn symbol indicates a post office.

In a time of rapid change it is difficult to ensure that all the information given is entirely accurate and up to date, and the possibility of error can never be completely eliminated. Although the publishers can accept no responsibility for inaccuracies and omissions, they are always grateful for corrections and suggestions for improvement.

2nd English edition

© Baedeker Stuttgart
Original German edition

© 1991 The Automobile Association
United Kingdom and Ireland

© 1991 Jarrold and Sons Ltd
English language edition worldwide

Distributed in the United Kingdom by the Publishing Division of The Automobile Association, Fanum House, Basingstoke, Hampshire, RG21 2EA.

The name *Baedeker* is a registered trademark
A CIP catalogue record for this book is available from the British Library

Licensed user:
Mairs Geographischer Verlag GmbH & Co., Ostfildern Kemnat bei Stuttgart

Printed in Italy by G. Canale & C. S.p.A – Borgaro T.se – Turin

0–7495–0287–8 UK

Contents

The Principal Sights at a Glance

This guide is concerned with the eastern Canary islands of Gran Canaria, Fuerteventura and Lanzarote. The western islands of Tenerife, Gomera and Hierro are described in the Baedeker/AA pocket guide "Tenerife".

Preface

This pocket guide to Gran Canaria, Fuerteventura and Lanzarote is one of the new generation of Baedeker guides.

Baedeker pocket guides, illustrated throughout in colour, are designed to meet the needs of the modern traveller. They are quick and easy to consult, with the principal places of interest described in alphabetical order, and the information is presented in a format that is both attractive and easy to follow.

The present guide is devoted to the eastern Canary Islands: in the first place Gran Canaria (Grand Canary), the most important and most visited island in the group, together with the two bare volcanic islands of Fuerteventura and Lanzarote, whose fantastic landscapes are now drawing increasing numbers of visitors. The guide is in three parts. The first part gives a general account of the islands, their geography, climate, flora and fauna, population, art, economy and transport, notable personalities, history and the culture of the early inhabitants. In the second part the places and features of tourist interest are described; and the third part contains a variety of practical information. Both the sights and the practical information are listed in alphabetical order.

The Baedeker pocket guides are noted for their concentration on essentials and their convenience of use. They contain numerous specially drawn plans and colour illustrations; and at the end of the book is a large map making it easy to locate the various places described in the "A to Z" section of the guide with the help of the coordinates given at the head of each entry.

Facts and Figures

General

This guide is concerned with the three larger islands of Gran Canaria, Fuerteventura and Lanzarote and the smaller islands of Alegranza, Graciosa and Lobos in the eastern part of the Canary Islands. The western islands of Tenerife, La Palma, Gomera and Hierro are described in the Baedeker/AA pocket guide "Tenerife".

Canary Islands

The Canary Islands (in Spanish Islas Canarias) are a group of seven major islands and six smaller ones in the Atlantic, lying between 100 and 300 km (60 and 190 miles) off the north-western coast of Africa (Morocco and western Sahara) and some 1100 km (700 miles) from the Spanish mainland (Cádiz), between latitude 27° 38' and 29° 35' N and between longitude 13° 20' and 18° 14' W. The whole archipelago extends for 500 km (300 miles) from east to west and 200 km (125 miles) from north to south. The islands have a total area of 7550 sq. km (2915 sq. km).

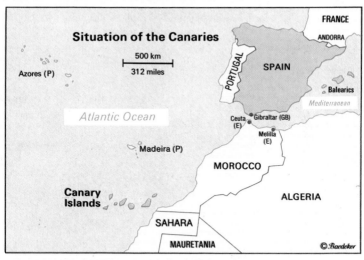

The eastern islands of Gran Canaria (area 1532 sq. km/592 sq. miles), Fuerteventura (1731 sq. km/668 sq. miles), Lanzarote (795 sq. km/307 sq. miles), Graciosa (27 sq. km/10.4 sq. miles), Alegranza (10 sq. km/3.9 sq. miles), Lobos (6 sq. km/2.3 sq. miles), Montaña Clara (1 sq. km/250 acres)

◀ *The Mountain village of Fataga*

9

and the two rocky islets of Roque del Oeste and Roque del Este (each 0.03 sq. km/7½ acres) form the province of Las Palmas de Gran Canaria (chief town Las Palmas). The province of Santa Cruz de Tenerife (chief town Santa Cruz) consists of the western islands of Tenerife (area 2057 sq. km/794 sq. miles), La Palma (728 sq. km/281 sq. miles, Gomera (378 sq. km/146 sq. miles) and Hierro (277 sq. km/107 sq. miles).

The two provinces make up the Autonomous Region of the Canary Islands (Comunidad Autónoma de Canarias), with Las Palmas and Santa Cruz alternating as capital of the region.

The Canary Islands are remarkable for the variety of their topography. Each of the islands has its own specific characteristics. Tenerife, with the highest peak in any of the Atlantic islands, the Pico de Teide (3718 m/12,199 ft), is commonly regarded as the most beautiful of the Canaries, and certainly none of the other islands has more striking scenery – on the one hand the bizarre stony desert of the Caldera de las Cañadas, on the other great expanses of pine forest and the fertile valleys in which bougainvilleas, poinsettias and hibiscus grow in such profusion. Tenerife, however, has one disadvantage: it has no large sandy beaches.

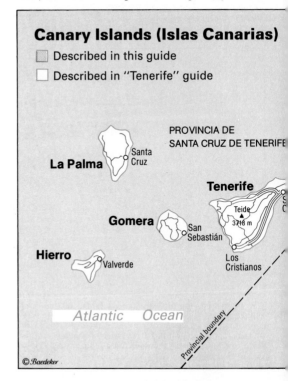

Canary Islands (Islas Canarias)

☐ Described in this guide

☐ Described in "Tenerife" guide

PROVINCIA DE
SANTA CRUZ DE TENERIFE

La Palma Santa Cruz

Tenerife

Teide ▲ 3718 m

Gomera San Sebastián

Hierro Valverde

Los Cristianos

Atlantic Ocean

Provincial boundary

© Baedeker

Only in the south of the islands are there a few small bays with stretches of beach; in the north bathers are dependent almost exclusively on man-made lidos, beautifully laid out though they are.

La Palma, Gomera and Hierro are no less attractive; but, having only small beaches of dark-coloured sand, they are not suitable for purely bathing holidays. In recent years Gomera has become a favourite haunt of adherents of the "alternative society"; La Palma and Hierro, untouched by mass tourism, are mainly visited by small numbers of independent travellers.

Gran Canaria draws greater numbers of visitors than the larger island of Tenerife. Although its scenery is less spectacular it has the great attraction of the beautiful sandy beaches in the south of the island and is well equipped with sport and entertainment facilities.

Those who want a more individual holiday will prefer Lanzarote, with smaller and quieter holiday resorts than Gran Canaria. Its extraordinary volcanic landscape and dazzlingly white little towns and villages have a particular charm.

In one respect Fuerteventura surpasses all the other islands. Its miles of beautiful beaches, many of them still almost unfrequented, offer ideal conditions for bathing and

sunbathing. This is the place for those who want to spend their holiday almost exclusively on the beach and to take advantage of the facilities for water sports and the other entertainments offered by the hotels.

Common features with other island groups

Together with the Azores, Madeira and the Cape Verde Islands the Canaries belong to the Macaronesian or Middle Atlantic Islands, which all show common features in flora and fauna, are all of volcanic origin and have similar topographical patterns.

Origins of the name

It is not known for certain how the Canaries got their name. The designation "Isla Canaria" appears for the first time on a Spanish chart of 1339. In antiquity the group was known as the Blessed or Fortunate Islands; later the name Canaria was applied by Pliny the Elder (A.D. 23–79) to the island now known as Gran Canaria. Pliny related the name (*canis* = dog) to the large dogs which lived on the island. There were certainly dogs in the Canaries in Pliny's time, though they were not unusually large. The Romans associated the islands with the kingdom of the dead which lay in the west; and it is possible that this had something to do with the name, for in ancient mythological conceptions the dead were conducted into the underworld by dogs. It has also been suggested that the bird known to the Romans as *canora* (singing bird) may have lived on the islands. Still another possibility is that the name may have come from the cape of Canauria (probably Cape Bojador) on the African coast.

Administration

The two provinces of the Canaries have governors appointed by the central government, with their headquarters in Santa Cruz and Las Palmas. The Cabildo Insular (Island Council) has, however, certain powers of self-government, with responsibility among other things for health services, roads, water supply and culture. Each island is divided into smaller administrative units (*municipios*), of which there are 21 on Gran Canaria, seven on Lanzarote and six on Fuerteventura. The lowest-ranking local authority is the *ayuntamiento*, or town-hall.

The Canaries were granted these powers of self-government in 1982 under the Spanish policy of decentralisation.

Independence movements

Many people in the Canaries feel that these powers of self-government are insufficient, and in recent years the degree of independence to be aimed at has been a principal theme of local political controversy. The Union of the Canarian People (Unión del Pueblo Canario, UPC) campaigns for complete independence, but is a long way from commanding a majority, and radical separatist organisations such as the Movement for Self-Determination and Independence (MPAIAC) find little popular support. A large proportion of the population would favour an extensive measure of self-government within a Spanish federal state. This appeals particularly to the poorer classes of the population, who suffer most from the economic crisis, and in their eyes the mainland Spaniards (the "Godos" or "Goths", as they are known in the Canaries) are responsible for all their troubles. Many of their grievances date from Franco's dictatorship, when the islands were scandalously neglected.

Formation of the Canaries

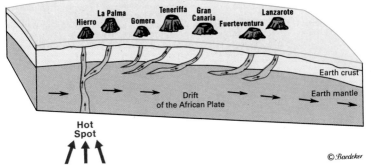

© *Baedeker*

In geological terms the Canary Islands are quite young. The age of the eastern islands of Lanzarote and Fuerteventura is estimated at between 16 and 20 million years and that of Gran Canaria between 13 and 14 million years, while the western islands are thought to have come into existence even later – Tenerife and Gomera perhaps between 8 and 12 million years ago, La Palma and Hierro only 2–3 million years ago. The variations in the topography of the individual islands confirm this picture of a reduction in age from east to west. Erosional forces have evidently been longer at work on Lanzarote and Fuerteventura with their low rounded hills than on the western Canaries with their rugged and mountainous terrain.

Origins of the archipelago

It is well established that all the islands are of volcanic origin, and the theory of "hot spots" has been put forward to explain how they came into being. At certain points in the earth's mantle – always the same points – magma collects in the course of millions of years and is then discharged in volcanic eruptions. A process of this kind gave rise in the first place to the islands of Lanzarote and Fuerteventura. As a result of continental drift, which is thought to take place in this region at a rate of between 2 and 3 cm (¾ and 1 in) a year, they moved gradually farther east. Magma then accumulated at the same spot and thrust its way upward to form other volcanic islands, ending with Hierro.

This theory is still the subject of controversy. What is certain, however, is that the earlier view that the Canaries, or at least Lanzarote and Fuerteventura, were once part of the African continent has been disproved.

There have been repeated volcanic eruptions in the Canaries, continuing into our own day; the most recent have been the eruptions on Tenerife in 1909 and on La Palma in 1949 and 1971. In 1730–36 and again in 1824 large areas on Lanzarote were devastated by volcanic eruptions. Gran Canaria and Fuerteventura have not suffered from volcanic action within historical times (the last eruption on Gran Canaria is believed to have taken place some 3000 years

Volcanic activity

13

ago), but both islands bear the mark of volcanic activity in earlier times. The topographical pattern of Fuerteventura and Lanzarote is set by volcanic cones of medium height, while Gran Canaria is dominated by the volcanoes in the centre of the island. The most striking volcanic phenomena are to be seen in the Parque Nacional de Timanfaya on Lanzarote, where, at the Islote del Hilario, temperatures of up to 400 °C (750 °F) are found only a few yards under the surface and a great range of different volcanic rocks can be seen in a kind of gigantic open-air geological museum.

The best known of the eruptive rocks is the bluish-black basalt. Trachyte is light coloured, with a rough surface; phonolite is greyish green. Obsidian, a dark-coloured glassy rock, is named after its discoverer, a Roman named Obsidius. Pumice, which has the astonishing property of floating in water, is a froth-like rock produced by the formation of gas bubbles in slow-flowing lava.

The expanses of infertile lava, often still looking quite fresh, are known as *malpaís* (badlands). After a period of weathering, however, the lava forms a soil which can be successfully cultivated if climatic conditions are favourable. Volcanic ash in particular contains nutrients essential for plant life. The people of the Canaries have learned by experience how to make the best use of the properties of the volcanic rock; thus pumice and lapilli (fragments of volcanic rock ranging in size between a pea and a walnut) are used to retain moisture in the soil (see Economy and Transport).

Topography of Gran Canaria

Gran Canaria, almost exactly circular in form, is the third largest island in the Canaries (after Tenerife and Fuerteven-

In the south of Gran Canaria: fertile barrancos and barren mountains

tura). The centre of the island is occupied by a range of mountains which reach their highest point in the Pozo de las Nieves (1949 m/6395 ft); but since this peak is surrounded by a number of other hills of almost the same height it does not dominate the island as Mt Teide dominates Tenerife. Characteristic of Gran Canaria are bizarrely shaped crags such as the Roque Nublo (1803 m/5916 ft), in which the harder rocks of former volcanic vents have been exposed by the erosion of the less resistant surrounding rock. The central mountain massif, also known as the Cumbre ("Summit"), divides the island into two very different landscape zones. While the hill slopes on the north are covered with a luxuriant growth of vegetation, the south side, with the exception of a few fertile valleys, is desertic in character. From the Cumbre deep wedge-shaped valleys (*barrancos*) run down to the coast. The largest of these gorges are on the west and south sides of Gran Canaria; the barrancos of Agaete, Aldea, Mogán and Fataga are particularly impressive. On the west side of the island the mountains fall steeply down to the coast; on the north side they merge into an upland region of medium height with a fringe of coastal cliffs. Only at the mouths of the barrancos are there narrow beaches of sand and stones. On the east and south sides of the island there are coastal plains bordered by sandy beaches, some of them of considerable size. The longest and most beautiful beaches are at Maspalomas and Playa del Inglés. It used to be thought that these extensive beaches and their fringes of dunes had been created by dust storms from the Sahara; but since the sand consists predominantly of carbonates it is now clear that it originated on the shelf surrounding the island itself, where upward movement of the land has given rise to beach terraces of varying height.

Gran Canaria has no perennial watercourses, but there are a number of productive springs on the island.

Fuerteventura and Lanzarote – known in antiquity as the Insulae Purpurariae because of the lichens which grew on the islands and were used to produce purple dye – are topographically very different from Gran Canaria and the western Canaries. Their desertic landscape is patterned by volcanic cones of medium height. Since they have no high hills there are no marked differences between their northern and southern halves due to the influence of the northeasterly trade winds (see Climate).

For a detailed description of the topography of Fuerteventura and Lanzarote, see the entries on those islands in the "A to Z" section of this guide.

Topography of Fuerteventura and Lanzarote

Climate

The Canaries have a warm temperate climate – milder and more agreeable than would normally be expected in these latitudes. It is mainly influenced by the trade winds, but also by the zone of high pressure over the Azores and the cool Canary Current.

General

The varying forms of relief in the individual islands give rise to certain climatic variations. On Lanzarote and

Fuerteventura, with hills rising no higher than 600–800 m (1970–2625 ft), the north-easterly trades have less influence on the weather than on Gran Canaria or the western Canaries. As a result these islands have a climate of desertic type (see A to Z, Fuerteventura and Lanzarote).

The weather can change very quickly in the Canaries but there are no long periods of bad weather. Even if the sun should disappear behind heavy clouds it is usually only necessary to travel a few miles to find a brilliantly blue sky again.

Temperatures

Temperature variations over the year are remarkably slight. Thus average temperatures in winter are around 19 °C (66 °F), while in summer the average is no more than 24 °C (75 °F) (see Practical Information, When to go). In the hills, of course, there is a temperature gradation according to altitude, and there are greater variations in temperature over the year. In July and August the weather pattern is sometimes affected by three- or four-day heat waves coming from the Sahara.

Water temperatures are around 19 °C (66 °F) in winter and 22 °C (72 °F) in summer.

Rainfall

Rainfall is mainly confined to the winter months, when it is brought by cyclones from northern latitudes. On Fuerteventura and Lanzarote there is sometimes no rain at all during the year, and in the south of Gran Canaria there is little rain even in winter. In the northern coastal region the annual rainfall is around 500 mm (20 in); at medium altitude it rises to 600–800 mm (24–31 in); and in the mountains it falls again. The snowline is about 1200 m (3900 ft), but as a rule only the Pozo de las Nieves, which rises to almost 2000 m (6500 ft), is covered with snow in winter.

Trade winds

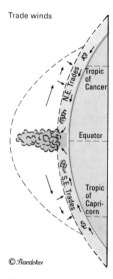

Over Gran Canaria, as over the western Canaries, a bank of cloud regularly forms at medium altitudes in the early morning, dispersing towards evening. The clouds rarely bring rain, but they do bring moisture in the form of mist and dew. The clouds are caused throughout almost the whole of the year by the trade winds blowing from the north-east, usually at force 4.

In contrast to other climatic influences, the trade winds are constant. Their circulation begins at the Equator, where the sun's warming influence on the earth is at its highest (the intra-tropical convergence, ITC). The warm air masses rise, becoming gradually cooler, and flow at a height of 12–15 km (7½–9½ miles) towards the Pole. After cooling still further they sink down to the surface of the earth in about latitude 30° and flow, close to the ground, towards the Equator. As a result of the rotation of the earth, however, the current of air is deflected from its original direction, flowing from the north-east in the Northern Hemisphere and from the south-east in the Southern Hemisphere. Above about 1500 m (4900 ft) the winds are warm and dry, below that altitude moist and rather cooler. So long as the separation between the upper and the lower layers (the "inversion" of the winds) is preserved there is little cloud formation; but when the winds come up against a sufficiently high hill the inversion is disturbed. The cool moist lower current is halted on the slopes exposed to the sun,

© Baedeker

becomes warmer and rises. It is then cooled again and condenses, and clouds form between 600 m (2000 ft) and 1700 m (5500 ft). (It follows that there is no formation of clouds during the night.)

With the trade winds blowing from the north-east, the southern parts of the islands are not affected in this way but are exposed only to warm dry winds blowing down from the hills.

The influence of the trade winds is less marked in winter. The sun's rays strike the Northern Hemisphere at a much more acute angle (whereas in the Southern Hemisphere the sun is vertically over the Tropic of Capricorn on 22 December). The zone subject to the trade winds then moves farther south, and the Canaries come under the influence of Atlantic troughs of low pressure.

Water supply has been a perennial problem in the Canaries, and with the increasing numbers of visitors in recent years the situation has become much worse. While Fuerteventura and Lanzarote (see A to Z, Fuerteventura and Lanzarote) have long had to contend with an acute shortage of fresh water, in the past Gran Canaria was able to ensure an adequate water supply by damming its rivers to form reservoirs. Nowadays, however, the reservoirs supplying the tourist resorts in the south of the island, with capacities of up to 40 million cu. m (8800 million gallons: Presa de Soria), are frequently dry, and more use has had to be made of ground-water supplies. The water is obtained by sinking wells, usually with a diameter of 3 m (10 ft) and a depth of between 150 and 200 m (500 and 650 ft), but sometimes going down to 300 m (1000 ft). As a result the water table has fallen in 20 years by more than 100 m (325 ft). Of the island's more than 2000 wells and springs over half are now dry. And to make matters worse, the more the water table falls the more sea water seeps in.

In spite of the gravity of the problem no agreement has yet been reached on alternative water supplies for Gran Canaria. The island's water resources are in the hands of a small number of private owners, who supply water to private consumers and hotels at high prices and are naturally reluctant to give up their monopoly. As a result the idea of bringing in large quantities of water by tanker from Madeira has had to be abandoned. It seems likely, therefore, that there will be increased dependence on the desalination of sea water, as already happens on Fuerteventura and Lanzarote. The desalination process, however, is not only bad for the environment but also expensive, involving the consumption of 6 litres (10½ pints) of oil for every 100 litres (22 gallons) of fresh water produced

Water supply

Flora and Fauna

Flora

The flora of the Canaries is unique in two respects. On the one hand there are found here within a relatively small area species of plants from almost every vegetation zone in the world; on the other hand there is a strikingly high

General

proportion of endemic species (plants which are found only here). Altogether the flora of the Canaries comprises almost 2000 species, fully 30 per cent of which are endemic. In the Mediterranean region, the Alps and southern Russia numerous fossils of fruits and leaves have been found which show that plants now occurring only in the Canaries were once common there too. The climatic catastrophes of the Late Tertiary era (the beginning of the Ice Age, the drying up of the Sahara) drove the subtropical flora of the period from its previous habitat, but the isolated situation of the Canaries allowed it to survive there. Moreover the considerable differences in altitude in the western Canaries and on Gran Canaria made it possible for plants to adapt to changing climatic conditions by migrating to different altitudes.

Vegetation zones

Major factors in the establishment of different vegetation zones have been differences in altitude and the influence of the trade winds.

The lowest level is arid and desertic, with a vegetation which includes the Canary date-palm and succulents such as the pillar euphorbia. This zone reaches up to as much as 1000 m (3300 ft) in the south of the islands but in the north is confined to the coastal regions. Here the natural vegetation includes junipers and the dragon tree between 200 m (650 ft) and 600 m (2000 ft), followed by laurels above 600 m. The zone of evergreen deciduous forest gives place at 1100 m (3600 ft) to the fayal-brezal formation (*faya* = bog myrtle, *brezo* = tree heath). The tree heath can grow to a height of 15 m (50 ft), but it may sometimes be no more than a shrub or even a dwarf shrub. The fayal-brezal formation together

Dragon tree

with the zone of laurel woodland is also known as the Monte Verde zone. In the northern half of the western Canaries the zone of pine forests begins at 1500 m (4900 ft), but in the south the Canary pine grows from 1000 m (3300 ft) upwards.

On Lanzarote and Fuerteventura, which have no hills higher than 600–800 m (2000–2600 ft) and thus do not benefit from the moist trade winds, there are no differences of vegetation zone. These islands as a whole are arid and support only scanty vegetation (see A to Z, Fuerteventura, Lanzarote).

Dragon tree

The most striking and most characteristic plant in the Canaries, with its tall stem and many-branched crown, is the dragon tree (*Dracaena draco*). It belongs to the Liliaceae and is closely related to the yucca. Some specimens grow to a height of 20 m (65 ft). The dragon tree's branches end in a cluster of long dark green sword-shaped leaves. Since the tree sends out shoots only after its first blossoming, there is little resemblance between a young tree and an older one like the mighty dragon tree of Icod. Dragon trees do not form annual rings, and the age of a tree can be determined only by the number of branches – an unreliable method, since the branches are put out at irregular intervals. For the indigenous inhabitants of the Canaries the dragon tree had special significance: they used the resin from its stem, which turned red on exposure to the air (dragon's blood), as an ingredient in their healing salves.

Canary date-palm

The Canary date-palm (*Phoenix canariensis*) has spread from the Canaries all over the Mediterranean. It is closely

Poinsettias

Date-palm

Succulents

Hibiscus

related to the date-palm of North Africa and the Arab countries, but is shorter and sturdier and has a fuller and more decorative crown with larger and more luxuriant leaves. The small dates it produces are woody and inedible. The finest examples of *Phoenix canariensis* are to be found in the south of Gran Canaria, in the Haría valley on Lanzarote and at Gran Tarajal on Fuerteventura.

Canary pine

The long and flexible needles of the Canary pine (*Pinus canariensis*) always occur in threes. Its hard reddish heartwood (Spanish *tea*) has long been (and still is) used in the construction of wooden ceilings and balconies. At the pine's altitude of between 1000 and 2000 m (3300 and 6600 ft) the moisture in the clouds brought by the trade winds condenses on its branches and drips down its needles into the ground. The water thus obtained is not merely sufficient for the tree's own needs but makes a substantial contribution to the island's water supply.

Prickly pear

A typical representative of the succulents is the prickly pear (*Opuntia ficus indica*), which was brought to the Canaries in the 16th c. It is commonly found on hillsides up to medium altitude. Its fruits are edible and are offered for sale. On this plant is reared the cochineal insect, which yields a red colouring substance; but cochineal is now produced commercially only on Lanzarote.

Ornamental plants

In addition to the prickly pear and some species of agave the Spanish conquerors also introduced to the Canaries a number of luxuriantly flowering ornamental plants, and oleanders, hibiscus and bougainvilleas are now to be seen in parks and gardens all over the islands. The red poinsettias, which form dense bushes 3–4 m (10–13 ft) high, are a ubiquitous feature of the landscape at many places on Gran Canaria. Particularly exotic is the strelitzia or bird-of-paradise flower with its unusual inflorescences.

The natural vegetation pattern of the islands was also altered by the introduction of various food plants, and the land at lower levels is now extensively planted with bananas, fruit trees, vegetables and vines.

Useful plants

The most important food crop on the islands is the banana. Since the end of the 19th c. a small species imported from Indochina (*Musa cavendishii*) which is not sensitive to weather, conditions has been cultivated in the Canaries.
The stem of the banana plant, made up of long, stiff, sappy sheaths, terminates in long fibrous leaves. When the plant is about a year old it produces a large club-shaped inflorescence, with the female flowers in the lower part and the male flowers in the upper part. Depending on the amount of sunshine and the altitude – bananas flourish in the Canaries up to 300–400 m (1000–1400 ft) – the fruit ripens in 4–6 months. A bunch of bananas weighs on average 25–30 kg (55–65 lb), and occasionally as much as 60 kg (130 lb). After bearing fruit the plant dies, but not before producing fresh shoots. The strongest of the shoots is preserved, and after another year puts forth a bud as long as a man's arm.

The banana

The felling of the islands' forests, beginning with the Spanish conquest and pursued on an increased scale since the end of the 19th c., has had devastating effects on ecological conditions. In the past great expanses of forest were cleared to provide land for cultivation: thus on Gran Canaria less than one per cent of the laurel woodland for which it was once famed has been preserved. In the last few decades efforts have been made on Gran Canaria and in the western Canaries to replant the forests, which are not only essential to the islands' water supply but also help to prevent erosion of the hillsides. At first eucalyptus trees were planted, but within the last 30 years or so it has mainly been pines – not the native Canary pine but a quick-growing species from North America, *Pinus insignis*.
The tourist boom and the extensive building developments associated with it have had serious consequences not only for the forests but for the rest of the islands' flora, and many endemic species are threatened with extinction. In the Jardín Canario on Gran Canaria these species are now being specially cultivated and wherever possible re-established in their original environment.

Environmental influences

Fauna

The fauna of the Canaries shows a much narrower range of species than their flora – though here, too, endemic species are relatively numerous.
There are no large mammals – only rabbits, hedgehogs and bats. It is reassuring for visitors that there are no scorpions or poisonous snakes. Lizards, however, are everywhere to be seen, and an occasional slow-worm, a lizard with

atrophied legs. The largest species of lizard is the 80 cm (30 in) long *Lacerta stehlinii*, which is endemic on Gran Canaria.

Birds are well represented – blackbirds, blue tits, a species of robin, chaffinches, woodpeckers, various species of pigeon, buzzards, kestrels, seagulls, ibises. Occasionally the fluting notes of the *capirote*, the Canary nightingale, can be heard. But visitors who expect to see the familiar yellow canary living in the wild in the islands from which it takes its name will be disappointed: there is only one inconspicuous wild form, the Canary finch, with greyish-green plumage and no great talent as a songster, from which the canary as we know it was bred.

There are innumerable endemic species of insects. Butterfly-lovers are well catered for; particularly striking are the Canary admiral and the brimstone, wih orange-red fore--wings.

The waters around the Canaries contain an abundance of fish. Salmon, cuttlefish, moray, bass, ray and sprat are merely a few of the numerous species represented. No dangerous sharks have been seen near the coast, but sometimes swarms of dolphins accompany the ferries.

Population

General

The Autonomous Region of the Canaries has a total population of 1.5 million, of whom some 660,000 live on Gran Canaria, 54,000 on Lanzarote and 30,000 on Fuerteventura. Of all the Canary Islands the most densely populated by a long way is Gran Canaria, with 439 people to the sq. kilometre (1137 to the sq. mile), compared with only 287 to the sq. kilometre (743 to the sq. mile) on the largest island, Tenerife. By far the largest concentration of population on Gran Canaria is in Las Palmas de Gran Canaria, the chief town, where something like half the island's inhabitants live.

The people of the Canaries are predominantly Roman Catholic, with only small minorities of Protestants.

It has been shown by anthropologists that the Canarians differ in a number of respects from other Spaniards, with many features that point to their descent from the indigenous inhabitants of the islands (see Early Inhabitants).

Social problems

After the end of the Franco dictatorship the social problems of the Canaries were very evident. It was estimated that at that time the illiteracy rate in some villages was as high as 50 per cent. It now averages between 8 and 12 per cent – still higher than in many other parts of Spain.

Unemployment is also higher than in mainland Spain. The number of registered unemployed in the Canaries is at present 120,000, but the real figure is likely to be considerably higher: at certain times of year something like a quarter of the population are believed to be unemployed. Depending on the length of time they have been in employment, they can expect to receive an unemployment allowance amounting to 48 per cent of their last pay for a period of 12 to 18 months.

In the past the usual way to escape from poverty was to emigrate, particularly to South America: there are said, for example, to be some 300,000 Canarians living in Caracas (Venezuela) alone. The South American states are now taking very few immigrants, and this has still further aggravated the unemployment problem in the Canaries. There is still, however, a shortage of skilled workers, since many of them have left for the Spanish mainland, attracted by the better prospects there.

As in the rest of Spain, Castilian (Castellano) is the language of government and business, and most Canarians also speak pure Castilian, though they tend, like the South Americans, to soften or elide the letter s. | Language

On Gran Canaria, Fuerteventura and Lanzarote English is spoken in the tourist areas, though in the remoter parts of the islands a smattering of Spanish will be found useful.

Art and Culture

Little is left of the art of the ancient Canarians. Apart from a few pieces of pottery and animal figures (see Early Inhabitants) visitors will find no artistic evidence of the indigenous culture of the archipelago. | Art and architecture

In the centuries following the Spanish conquest numbers of churches and modest public buildings were erected, closely following European and particularly Spanish architectural and artistic traditions. Although there are no outstanding masterpieces there are some buildings of notable quality, in very varying styles.

At first Gothic influences can be detected (e.g. in the ribbed vaulting of the Catedral de Santa Ana in Las Palmas), and Gothic architectural forms sometimes incorporate Renaissance features (Casa de Colón, Las Palmas).

The Mudéjar style, which shows a mingling of Moorish with Gothic or Renaissance forms, was developed in Spain by the Mudéjars (the "Moors who were allowed to stay"), and also by Christian architects influenced by the Moorish style. Its main characteristics are horseshoe arches, stalactitic vaulting and stucco ornament.

The Mudéjar style developed into Plateresque, which came into vogue in Spain at the end of the 15th c. In this style the façades of buildings were covered with a profusion of intricate ornament. A particular variant of the style developed in the Canaries, and many buildings were given ceilings of Canary pine, richly carved and sometimes painted.

In the 17th c. Baroque came to the Canaries, but in architecture at least was less widely diffused than Gothic and Renaissance. Many churches, however, were equipped with Baroque furnishings and works of art.

The neo-classical style which came in during the second half of the 18th c. left its mark mainly on the façades of buildings, which were strictly articulated and, in comparison with Baroque architecture, given little in the way of sculptural decoration (façade of Catedral de Santa Ana, Las Palmas).

The characteristic feature of 19th c. architecture is the mingling of a variety of styles modelled on the buildings of the past.

A typical wooden balcony

Wood-framed windows

Since the 1960s there has been a regular building boom on Gran Canaria, and innumerable huge hotel complexes have been built, particularly in the south of the island. New tourist resorts like Maspalomas/Playa del Inglés have been created, and the process is continuing. These developments, often of questionable architectural quality, have given rise to some controversy on the islands. Some attempts have been made to give new developments a more human face, particularly by the Canarian architect César Manrique (see Notable Personalities), who has largely been successful in preserving his native island of Lanzarote from being spoiled by modern building.

In all periods the Canaries have been notable for fine wood-carving. In most of the major churches in the archipelago there are statues in wood by the greatest Canarian sculptor, Luján Pérez (1756–1815). Mention has already been made of the richly decorated wooden ceilings to be found in both sacred and secular buildings. Perhaps the most typical features of Canarian architecture, however, are the beautiful wooden balconies. A stroll through the old part of Las Palmas (Vegueta) or the little town of Teror will reveal numbers of these narrow little balconies, all with different forms of decoration.

Folk traditions

An essential part in the life of the Canarians is played by their fiestas. As a rule these are of religious origin and are held in honour of one of the island saints. They usually begin with a religious procession, which is followed by more secular diversions.

Music features largely in these ceremonies. The songs, passionate in rhythm and melody, are usually accompanied on the *timple,* a small stringed instrument.

In almost every place of any size there is a ring for Canarian wrestling contests (lucha canaria). In this ring, 9–10 m (30–33 ft) in diameter, the contest is between two wrestlers, each belonging to a 12-man team. The fight lasts for a maximum of three three-minute rounds, and the winner is the first to achieve a fall.

Traditional sports

The *juego del palo,* a contest like singlesticks but played with two sticks, calls for extraordinary dexterity. Each contestant has to attack his opponent and ward off his blows, while moving the body as little as possible.

Economy and Transport

In the course of their history the Canaries have exported a variety of agricultural products. In antiquity the *Rocella* lichen which grew on Lanzarote and Fuerteventura was in great demand, since it was used to produce a valuable purple dye (hence the name of Insulae Purpurariae given to the two easterly Canary Islands). After the Spanish conquest sugar-cane was grown on the islands, but as a result of competition from the cheaper sugar of Central America this branch of the economy was already in decline in the 16th c. The main crop then became wine, and in the 17th and

Agriculture

Prickly pears

A "hand" of bananas

18th c. the heavy Malvasía (Malmsey) of the Canaries was much prized at European courts. But tastes changed, and in the 19th c. there was a switch to the rearing of the cochineal insect, a parasite yielding a red colouring substance which flourished on the newly planted fields of prickly pear. With the development of aniline dyes. however, the economic importance of the cochineal insect declined, and cochineal is now used only in the manufacture of lipsticks and for colouring aperitifs, aerated drinks and sweets. The cochineal insect is still reared on a small scale on Lanzarote.

The ailing economy of the islands was then given a boost by the cultivation of the banana – a small species (*Musa cavendishii*), less vulnerable to weather conditions, which was brought in from Indochina and by about 1890 was being grown on a considerable scale on Gran Canaria and the western Canaries. But in recent years banana-growing, too, has been in a state of crisis. Since the small Canary banana, tasty though it is, looks puny in comparison with its competitors from Central and South America, it is now almost unsaleable on the European market, and the costs of production are much higher than in other countries. The Spanish government has, therefore, been compelled to subsidise Canary bananas by guaranteeing a market, and 96 per cent of the total crop (some 400,000 tonnes) goes to the Spanish mainland. This, however, is only a temporary solution. Since Spain has become a member of the EEC a ten-year transitional period for the Canary banana has been agreed, after which bananas from other countries are to be admitted to the Spanish market.

The cultivation of pot-plants, an alternative to bananas

The people of the Canaries are now beginning to adjust to the new economic situation. Banana plantations are increasingly giving place to exotic vegetables, cut flowers and pot plants; a number of experimental pineapple plantations, for example, are now operating successfully in the western Canaries.

Banana-growing is now concentrated in the northern half of Gran Canaria, where it thrives up to a height of about 400 m (1300 ft). At higher levels the main crops are potatoes, grain, maize, sugar-cane (chiefly around Arucas), cabbages, figs and other kinds of fruit. In the south-east and south-west of the island the principal crop is tomatoes, and Gran Canaria is the largest producer of tomatoes for the European market in the Canaries. Crops for export are produced mainly between November and May. Excellent wine is produced on Gran Canaria (in the Tafira area) and Lanzarote, which is particularly noted for its Malvasía.

While the banana plantations and tomato fields on Gran Canaria depend on expensive irrigation schemes, on Lanzarote and Fuerteventura dry-farming methods are used. The soil is covered or mixed with volcanic lapilli and pumice, which, being porous, are able to store water. They also increase condensation immediately above the ground, since they take in heat during the day and cool rapidly at night. Thanks to these special properties they keep the soil perpetually moist to a depth of 25–30 cm (10–12 in).

Stock-farming is of secondary importance, and locally reared cattle and pigs meet only part of the islands' requirements. The stock-farming centre of Gran Canaria is Telde. The cows are mostly kept in cowsheds, since they would be liable to injure themselves on the rough terrain. Herds of goats are a ubiquitous feature of the landscape, particularly on Fuerteventura. Dromedaries are still used as working animals.
Fishing (particularly tunny-fishing) is practised around all the islands.

In general agriculture, once the main means of subsistence, is now declining in importance, accounting for barely 10 per cent of the gross domestic product. The production of foodstuffs covers only 25 per cent of local consumption.

Industry contributes about 25 per cent of the gross domestic product. It concentrates mainly on food-processing, but there are also a number of medium-sized woodworking, papermaking and fish-canning plants and factories producing building materials and fertilisers. Craft goods (embroidery, etc.) are produced in h small establishments – some very small indeed.

Industry

Since 1852 the Canaries have been a free trade (duty-free) zone, and this has given a great boost to trade. Shortage of water, raw materials and electric power, however, put a brake on economic development, and as a result the balance of trade has long been in deficit. Imports, principally from mainland Spain, are increasing, and there are also considerable imports from West Germany (beer, milk, butter, fruit juices, etc.).

Commerce

Puerto de la Luz, Las Palmas

Transport

In line with the development of tourism there have been considerable improvements in the road systems of the eastern Canaries. On Fuerteventura and Lanzarote all towns and villages of any size can be reached on well-built roads. On Gran Canaria the motorway linking Las Palmas with the south of the island cannot always cope with the heavy traffic, and there are sometimes long tailbacks, particularly at the end of the improved section of road, just before Maspalomas. In the north of the island traffic now flows smoothly along the new coast road completed in 1983. In the west the roads are good but there are many bends. There are no railways in the Canaries, and public transport is confined to buses.

There are regular ferry services between the islands, and Las Palmas's harbour (Puerto de la Luz) plays a major part in the economy of the archipelago, as well as being a key point in Spain's overseas trade.

Gran Canaria has an international airport, the Aeropuerto de Gando. The airports on Fuerteventura and Lanzarote handle only domestic flights and international charter flights.

Tourism

The first holiday visitors – mainly from Britain and Scandinavia – came to Gran Canaria in the 1950s, staying in Las Palmas or in the parador at the Cruz de Tejeda. In the late sixties and early seventies, with the development of the large tourist centre of Maspalomas/Playa del Inglés, there was a dramatic increase in the number of visitors to Gran Canaria, and Fuerteventura and Lanzarote also began to feature in the tourist trade. Tourism now accounts for 67 per cent of the gross domestic product. 1½ million foreign visitors (mainly Germans) come to Gran Canaria every year, 550,000 (mainly from Britain) to Lanzarote, nearly 200,000 (almost exclusively from Germany) to Fuerteventura. In addition numbers of mainland Spaniards come to enjoy the "eternal spring" of the Canaries.

While annual growth rates of more than 10% were the norm until 1988, this trend has been reversed during the last two years; in 1989 the number of visitors arriving by air showed a reduction of 10.7% compared with the previous year.

Notable Personalities

Jean de Béthencourt
(1359–1426)

Jean de Béthencourt, a Norman, was entrusted by Henry III of Castile with the task of conquering the Canaries. His lieutenant was Gadifer de la Salle, with whom he had taken part in a "crusade" against Tunis in 1390.

The two men assembled an expeditionary fleet, which sailed from La Rochelle in 1402. When Béthencourt at last saw the first islands in the archipelago he named them in delight, bare and rocky though they were, Alegranza (Joy) and Graciosa (the Beautiful). Soon afterwards the adventurers landed on Lanzarote and were able to capture it in a relatively short time. Then Béthencourt returned to Spain for reinforcements, and Henry bestowed on him the title of "king of the Canary Islands": whereupon Gadifer, offended, took no further part in the enterprise. In consequence Béthencourt was solely responsible for the conquest of Fuerteventura, which was achieved in 1405, and gave the name of Betancuria to the town which he founded as its capital. Soon afterwards he also took Hierro. Thereafter he settled the two islands with peasants from Normandy and Spain, and the native population was rigorously converted to Christianity. Béthencourt then tried to subjugate the islands of Gran Canaria and La Palma as well, but the resistance of the natives proved too much.

In 1406 Béthencourt appointed his nephew Maciot de Béthencourt viceroy of the islands and returned to France, where he died in 1425 in his castle in Granville.

José Clavijo y Fajardo
(1730–1806)

José Clavijo y Fajardo was born on Lanzarote and educated in a Dominican monastery on the island, where he studied law and philosophy as well as theology. He then went to Madrid, where he attracted some public interest with a work on Spanish military affairs. Thereafter he became even better known as editor, from 1762 onwards, of "El Pensador", a periodical promoting the ideas of the Enlightenment. He fell temporarily into disgrace on account of a love affair with Louise Caron, sister of the dramatist Beaumarchais, who challenged him to a duel for his infidelity. The incident soon blew over, however, and Clavijo was appointed director of the Theatre Royal; even Beaumarchais was reconciled with him after "The Barber of Seville" was performed in Madrid as a result of his intervention. He was also a friend of Buffon and Voltaire.

Christopher Columbus
(1451–1506)

Christopher Columbus (in Spanish Cristóbal Colón, in Italian Cristoforo Colombo), a native of Genoa, visited the Canaries several times on his voyages of discovery.

Columbus went to Lisbon in 1476 hoping to get assistance for his project of seeking a western route to India; then, proving unsuccessful, applied to Spain in 1485. It was not until 1492, however, that Ferdinand of Aragon and his wife Isabella of Castile signed an agreement with Columbus making him viceroy of any lands he discovered and granting him 10 per cent of the expected profits.

On his first voyage (1492–93) Columbus put in at Gran Canaria. It is uncertain where he anchored, whether in the area of present-day Puerto de la Luz (Las Palmas) or in

Jean de Béthencourt

Columbus

Miguel de Unamuno y Jugo

Gando Bay. He had his ships overhauled and took on supplies of water and provisions. During his stay he lived in the house which still bears his name, the Casa de Colón in Calle de Colón. At the end of August he set out for Gomera, and his logbook records that when sailing past Tenerife he observed an eruption of Mount Teide. During his stay on Gomera he met Beatriz de Bobadilla, wife of Hernán Peraza the Younger (see History, p. 35); but whether he had a liaison with her, as rumour had it, is uncertain.

On his second voyage (1493–96) Columbus spent only one day on Gran Canaria; on his third (1498–1500) he only called in at Gomera.

On his fourth crossing of the Atlantic (1502–04) Columbus again took on supplies on Gran Canaria. On his return from this voyage he was a sick man, and he died in Valladolid in 1506.

Visitors to the Canaries will frequently come across the work of the architect, painter and sculptor César Manrique, a native of Lanzarote. The buildings and developments for which he has been responsible, such as the Costa de Martiánez, a bathing complex and seafront promenade in Puerto de la Cruz (Tenerife), have left a distinctive mark on the Canaries. After some early exhibitions of his work in the Canaries Manrique moved in 1945 to Madrid, where he studied at the Academy of Fine Art. Thereafter he achieved further success in the field of abstract painting, and his work was exhibited not only in Spain but in many cities in Europe, Japan and the United States. In 1965, now with an international reputation, he went to New York to take up a post in the International Institute of Art Education. In 1968 he returned to Lanzarote and built himself a house near Arrecife, in a barren volcanic landscape. From the very original rooms of the house spiral staircases lead down into the natural volcanic caves beneath. It was designed to serve as a model of the kind of house which it would be possible to build at many places on the island.

In 1968 Manrique founded the Museum of Contemporary Art on Lanzarote, and in subsequent years he was concerned in numerous building projects in the Canaries, particularly on Lanzarote (Jameos del Agua, Costa Teguise,

César Manrique
(b. 1920)

Palacio de Spínola in Teguise, etc.) and Tenerife. Basing himself on native architectural traditions, he seeks to preserve the landscape as it is; architecture should be in harmony with its setting. He sees it as his principal task to save his native island of Lanzarote from over-building. In this he has been successful, for there is only a single high-rise block on Lanzarote and the bizarre landscape of the island remains unspoiled by electricity pylons or advertising signs.

Benito Pérez Galdós (1843–1920)

Benito Pérez Galdós is the most celebrated writer born in the Canaries. The house in Las Palmas (Gran Canaria) in which he was born and spent his early years is now a museum. Little is known about these years on Gran Canaria. He was the youngest of the many children of an officer in fairly comfortable circumstances. After finishing his schooling in Las Palmas in 1863 he was sent to Madrid to study law and lived there, apart from many visits to different European countries, for the rest of his life. He returned only once to the Canaries, and the islands play little part in his works, the most important of which are the "Episodios nacionales", a series of 46 volumes recounting in semi-fictional form the history of Spain in the 19th century. He was continually fascinated by the city of Madrid, and in his "Recollections of a Man without a Memory" writes, "I pass over my childhood, for it is of no interest, or at least is scarcely distinguishable from the experiences of my years of more or less diligent study."
A controversial figure in his lifetime as a representative of Spanish liberal thought, Pérez Galdós is now recognised in Spain as the leading novelist of modern times.

Néstor Martín Fernández de la Torre (1887–1938)

The painter Néstor Martín Fernández de la Torre, born on Gran Canaria on 7 February 1887, is commemorated by the museum in Las Palmas which bears his name.
After studying at the Academy of Fine Art in Madrid he travelled widely in Europe and while in London made a special study of the Pre-Raphaelites. He first achieved artistic success in 1908, and in subsequent years painted many pictures showing the influence of Symbolism which were hung in international exhibitions. He also painted a number of murals, like those in the Teatro Pérez Galdós in Las Palmas and the Casino in Santa Cruz de Tenerife. These huge compositions depict the people of the Canaries, often in rather idealised form.
In 1934 Néstor de la Torre launched a great campaign aimed at a revival of Canarian folk traditions and architecture. He conceived the idea of the Pueblo Canario, the Canarian Village, in Las Palmas, though the project, based on his watercolour paintings, was not carried out until 1939, a year after his death. In 1956, thanks to the munificence of the painter's brothers, the Néstor Museum was opened in the Pueblo Canario.

Miguel de Unamuno y Jugo (1864–1936)

Although the Spanish writer and philosopher Miguel de Unamuno y Jugo is commemorated by a huge monument on the Montaña Quemada on Fuerteventura, he spent only a short time on the island – and then against his will.
Unamuno, then Rector of the University of Salamanca, was exiled to Fuerteventura in 1924 for opposing the military

dictatorship of General Primo de Rivera. He decided to go into exile without his family: as he wrote at the time, he needed solitude. He arrived on Fuerteventura on 10 March 1924. In the subsequent months the extraordinary landscape of the island must have made a strong impression on him: he describes Fuerteventura as an "oasis in the desert of civilisation" and as "a naked, arid, barren, bone-hard land which soothes the spirit." The solitude which Unamuno found on Fuerteventura in abundant measure fostered his spiritual bent but also, as his work shows, strengthened his religious doubts.

In July 1924, with the help of his eldest son, Unamuno left Fuerteventura and fled to Paris. A few months after his flight became known the Spanish government rehabilitated him. He did not return to Spain, however, but continued to live in voluntary exile in France. In 1930 he finally went back to Spain, and in 1931 resumed his teaching at Salamanca University.

History

From 3000 B.C.	The Canaries are believed to have been settled by at least two waves of incomers. The first human type to reach the islands has more Cro-Magnon characteristics than later arrivals, who show Mediterranean features. The history of these first inhabitants (see Early Inhabitants), living almost totally isolated from the rest of the world, is obscure. There are no written records – apart from some rock inscriptions which have not been deciphered - until the Spanish conquest in the 15th c.
From 1100 B.C.	Other ancient peoples are aware of the existence of the Canary archipelago. In the course of their exploratory voyages along the West African coast the Phoenicians and later the Carthaginians visit the islands, but no regular trading contacts develop.
Between 25 B.C. and A.D. 23	King Juba II of Mauretania (25 B.C.–A.D. 23) sends ships to the Canaries, which, on the evidence of Pliny the Elder, they seem to have reached.
1st c. A.D.	Pliny the Elder (A.D. 23–79) mentions the islands in his "Natural History" and gives their names, together with information about dimensions and distances which is not in accordance with the facts.
2nd c. A.D.	The Greek geographer Ptolemy (c. A.D. 100–160) shows the islands on his map of the world – the first map to give degrees of longitude. He makes the prime meridian (the end of the then known world) pass through the western tip of Hierro, the Punta de Orchilla.
End of 13th c.	The Canaries, having fallen into oblivion for many centuries, are rediscovered by European seafarers questing for slaves.
1312	The Genoese seaman Lancelot Maloisel (Lanzarotto Malocello) cruises in the Canaries and lands on the island later to be named after him, Lanzarote. He retains possession of the island until 1330.
1340–42	The Portuguese and Spaniards send ships to the Canaries, many of them from Majorca. Since they are usually heavily armed and carry horses, the objective is probably not merely trade.
1344	Pope Clement VI, as having authority over "all lands to be discovered", appoints Luis de la Cerda, a scion of the Spanish royal family, king of the Canary Islands – though this title does not imply possession of the land.
End of 14th c.	Roberto de Bracamonte succeeds Luis de la Cerda but, like him, is content with the purely theoretical title of king and makes no attempt to conquer the islands. He leaves this task to his cousin Jean de Béthencourt (1359–1425: see Notable Personalities).

Together with the Spanish nobleman Gadifer de la Salle (*c.* 1340–1422) Jean de Béthencourt makes the first attempt to win the Canaries for the Spanish Crown. After occupying Lanzarote Béthencourt is granted the title of king of the Canary Islands. Gadifer de la Salle takes no part in further conquests after his claim to the title is rejected.

1402

Béthencourt conquers the islands of Fuerteventura and Hierro but fails in his attempts to take Gran Canaria and La Palma. He returns to France in 1406.

1405

Béthencourt appoints his nephew Maciot de Béthencourt viceroy of the islands. In 1415, on the intervention of the king, Maciot is compelled to retire on the ground of incompetence, but sells his office successively to the royal envoy Diego de Herrera, Prince Henry of Portugal and a Spanish count, Hernán Peraza the Elder. The situation about possession of the islands thus becomes thoroughly confused, and in subsequent years ships are sent both by Spaniards and by Portuguese to conquer them.

1406–15

The first episcopal see in the Canaries is established on Lanzarote.

1419

Hernán Peraza the Elder, who hitherto has alternated between Fuerteventura, Hierro and Gomera, finally establishes his authority on Gomera. He and his successors rule the island with ruthless disregard of the interests of the inhabitants.

1445

The Spanish Crown buys back the right of sovereignty over the islands of Fuerteventura, Lanzarote, Gomera and Hierro.

1478

When a Spanish force led by Juan Rejón lands on Gran Canaria in 1478 the island is ruled by two kings or *guanartemes*, as they are called. Tenesor Semidan, who controls the western part of the island, has his seat at Gáldar, while Doramas rules the eastern half from Telde. In 1478 the Spaniards found the town of Las Palmas, which becomes their base for further conquest. They win a decisive victory, capture Tenesor Semidan and ship him and his retinue to Spain, where he is baptised and thereafter sides with the Spaniards. In spite of this it takes much bitter fighting under the leadership of Pedro de Vera and Alonso Fernández de Lugo before the native peoples are finally subdued.

1478–83

The Treaty of Alcáçovas settles Spanish and Portuguese territorial claims: the Canary Islands are recognised as Spanish, and Portugal is compensated by the whole of West Africa and various offshore islands.

1479

On his first voyage of discovery Columbus (in Spanish Cristóbal Colón: see Notable Personalities) puts in at Gran Canaria and then at Gomera. On his later voyages (1493, 1498 and 1502) he calls in several times at these islands and once at Hierro.

1492

Alonso Fernández de Lugo, an Andalusian noble, lands on La Palma and establishes his authority over the whole island.

1492–93

History

1494–96	Alonso Fernández de Lugo gradually conquers the whole of Tenerife, which has preserved its independence longer than any other of the Canary Islands. The island then, like Gran Canaria and La Palma, becomes directly subject to the Spanish Crown. Supreme authority is exercised by *capitanes generales* (captains-general), who allocate the usufruct (exploitation without ownership) of land and sell water rights. Gomera, Hierro, Lanzarote and Fuerteventura have the status of *señorios*. The Spanish Crown has sovereignty over these islands but grants right of possession – in effect fiefs – to nobles and ecclesiastics, subject to duties payable to the rulers of the islands and to the Spanish Crown.
16th–17th c.	The indigenous population of the Canaries – apart from those who have been sold as slaves – gradually become assimilated to the Spanish conquerors. The islands rapidly acquire economic importance through the cultivation of sugar-cane and later the production of wine. Their new-found wealth, however, attracts many pirates. The British, Dutch and Portuguese make repeated attempts to take Las Palmas, but their attacks are beaten off.
1537	After the Spanish conquest slavery is prohibited, but the ban is frequently evaded, as is shown by a later decree by Pope Paul III making slavery a punishable offence.
1730–36	In a series of violent volcanic eruptions large areas of Lanzarote are devastated.
1799	In the course of his voyage to South America the explorer and naturalist Alexander von Humboldt (1769–1859) cruises in Canarian waters and spends some time on Tenerife (see Quotations).
1820	Las Palmas becomes capital of Gran Canaria.
1822	Santa Cruz de Tenerife becomes capital of the whole archipelago.
1824	Further volcanic eruptions on Lanzarote.
1837	The *señorio* status of Fuerteventura, Lanzarote, Gomera and Hierro is abolished.
1852	Queen Isabella II declares the Canaries a free trade zone.
1882	The development of the harbour of Las Palmas (Puerto de la Luz) is begun, under the engineer León y Castillo.
End of 19th c.	The cultivation and export of bananas becomes the mainstay of the Canarian economy.
1912	The islands are granted local self-government. Cabildos Insulares (Island Councils) are established.
1927	The Canary Islands are divided into two provinces, Santa Cruz de Tenerife (Tenerife, Gomera, Hierro and La Palma) and Las Palmas de Gran Canaria (Gran Canaria, Lanzarote and Fuerteventura).

General Francisco Franco (1892–1975), commander of the military region of the Canaries, meets his senior officers in the Bosque de la Esperanza, on the island of Tenerife, to plan the military coup which leads to the Spanish Civil War (1936–39). 1936

Volcanic eruption (Volcán de Teneguía) on La Palma, the most recent eruption in the Canaries. 1971

After Franco's death Juan Carlos becomes king of Spain. 1975

Bomb attacks by Canarian separatists, supported by the Algerian government, under the slogan "Fuera Godos" ("Goths out" – the "Goths" being the mainland Spaniards). There are no serious injuries in the attacks, which are supported by the government of Algeria. 1976–78

A new democratic constitution comes into force; Spain becomes a constitutional monarchy. 1978

The Canary Islands, together with the other sixteen "autonomous regions" of Spain, get their own regional constitution and elected representative bodies. 1982

The elected assembly of the Canaries opposes Spanish entry to the European Community, fearing that Canary fruit and vegetables will not be competitive on the European market. 1985

On 1 January Spain becomes a member of the EEC; there is a special agreement on the Canaries. 1986

In December the Canarian Parliament passes a bill approving the islands' full membership of the EEC. 1989

Early Inhabitants

Their name

The name Guanches is frequently but erroneously applied to the indigenous inhabitants of the Canaries. Strictly, however, the term applies only to the inhabitants of Tenerife: the word Guanche in the old Canarian language means "son of Tenerife" (from *guan* = son, *Achinech* = Tenerife). The original population of the other islands had different names. In this section, therefore, the early inhabitants of the Canaries as a whole are referred to not as Guanches but as ancient Canarians.

Origin

The origin of the ancient Canarians is still an enigma. The "catastrophe theory" of some early geologists, who believed that the Canaries had been separated from the African continent together with some surviving inhabitants, is no longer tenable. The first inhabitants of the islands must, therefore, have reached them by boat, although no remains of any such craft have so far been found.

It is established, however, that the ancient Canarians belonged to two different racial types. A considerable proportion were of Cro-Magnon race (named after the type site in France), with long skulls, broad faces, high foreheads and short narrow noses. The Spanish chroniclers describe the inhabitants of the Canaries as tall and broad-shouldered, with fair hair and light-coloured eyes. There was also another race, taller and more slender, and of Mediterranean type. It is assumed, therefore, that the islands were settled by at least two waves of incomers.

Since Fuerteventura lies only 100 km (60 miles) off the African mainland, the first settlers could have come from there. This theory finds support in the fact that there are still people living in north-west Africa who belong to the Cro-Magnon type. Moreover, with the normal currents and trade winds, a boat leaving the coast of what is now Morocco would be driven south past the Canaries. On the other hand it was much easier, in spite of the greater distance, to reach the archipelago from the Iberian peninsula. The ancient Canarians, therefore, were not necessarily descended from the prehistoric inhabitants of north-west Africa. There may also have been connections with the Atlantic coast of western Europe. Such evidence as we have of the culture of the ancient Canarians (megalithic petroglyphs, forms of religion, etc.) suggests possible affinities with the megalithic culture.

There remains the question of when the settlement of the Canaries took place. The ancient Canarians had no knowledge of metals, and their remains suggest that contact with other peoples must have been broken off as early as the Neolithic period. Some authorities believe that the first settlers reached the archipelago about 3000 B.C. It is unlikely that there were any major waves of immigration after 1000 B.C.

Cultural level

The ancient Canarians were herdsmen and primitive tillers of the soil. On land cleared from the forest they grew barley and wheat, and also pulses, without the aid of the plough. Their domestic animals were goats, sheep, pigs and dogs.

Cenobio de Valerón, Gran Canaria

They lived mainly in caves, which suited the climatic conditions of the time. The interiors of the caves were often hewn smooth, and sometimes had thatched reed ceilings. Artificial caves were sometimes hewn from the rock; the Cenobio de Valerón on Gran Canaria is an example of an elaborate system of inter-connected cave chambers. There were also occasional stone structures, particularly tombs (tumulus of Gáldar on Gran Canaria), roofed semi-underground dwellings and thatch-roofed wattle-and-daub huts.

Dwellings

The staple food was *gofio* – roasted barley, ground into a powder, mixed with honey and water and rolled into balls (see Practical Information, Food and drink). Other important foodstuffs were goat-meat, milk and butter. Mushrooms and wild fruits were gathered in the forests. Fish and seafood must also have featured on the menu – though, lacking boats, the ancient Canarians could fish only in waters just off the coast.

Food

The clothing of the ancient Canarians was primitive. A common garment was the *tamarco*, a cloak made by joining goatskins with thorns from plants. The art of weaving was unknown, although there were sheep on the islands. Garments were also made of plaited palm fibres and bast.

Clothing

When the Spaniards conquered the Canaries in the 15th c. they had little difficulty in overcoming the inhabitants, who had only the most primitive weapons. The bow and arrow were unknown to them, and their only means of defence were stones, fire-hardened throwing spears and wooden

Tools and weapons

39

clubs. For hand-to-hand fighting they had thin pointed stone blades, so sharp that they could also be used for cutting up objects. They had no metal tools or weapons, and lacked even the ground stone axes of the Neolithic period.

Social structure

That the ancient Canarians, in spite of these living conditions, were not entirely primitive cave-men is shown by their social structure. There were three classes of society – the king and his family, the nobles and the rest of the population. There seems to have been no clear distinction between the second and third groups. Nobility was not hereditary but could be attained by personal qualities, and noble status had to be confirmed by the priests. On the individual islands there were independent tribal territories under the overlordship of the king. Gran Canaria was ruled by two kings, known as *guanartemes*: one, in the western half of the island, had his seat at Gáldar, while the other ruled the eastern half from Telde.

Inheritance was in the female line, but it was not a matriarchal society. A woman could not herself exercise royal authority, but her husband was authorised by her election to rule. In practice the system of inheritance in the female line gave women a high status in society, and there is some evidence that women played a major part in religious rites. On Fuerteventura two women are said to have taken the leading role in legal and religious matters.

Religion

The ancient Canarians believed in a single all-powerful higher being. On Gran Canaria it was Acoran (the Greatest or Highest). An important part was played in the religious practices of the ancient Canarians by sacred mountains and cave sanctuaries, where animal sacrifices and libations were made to the god.

Burial practices

To the ancient Canarians the world of the dead was closely bound up with the world of the living. Dwellings and burial-places cannot always be clearly distinguished from one another, for both natural and man-made caves were used either for living in or for burial. Only on Gran Canaria have burial mounds been found.

The bodies of the higher classes of the population were mummified by being anointed with goat's-milk butter and preserved by the application of heat and smoke. The brain was never removed; nor, normally, the entrails. Compared with Egyptian methods this was a very primitive form of mummification, and in spite of the dry climate the mummies soon decomposed. Evidently the caves traditionally used for burial were repeatedly reoccupied. The mummies found in such caves and now displayed in the museums of Las Palmas de Gran Canaria and Santa Cruz de Tenerife are none of them very old; they were probably embalmed about the 10th or 11th c.

Language

Only scanty remnants of the language of the ancient Canarians have survived into our day, mainly in the form of place-names. It has been suggested, on the basis of this evidence, that the Canarian tongue was related to the language of the Berbers. It may be, however, that Berber elements entered the language at some later date. The various

An ancient Canarian mummy

islands had different dialects, though basic words were common to them all.

When the Spaniards conquered the Canaries the native population had no written script. Many rock inscriptions, however, have been found on the islands, some of them quite recently. The first such inscriptions were discovered in 1867 on La Palma (Cueva Belmaco); then in 1870 there was found on Hierro (Los Letreros) a rock face with inscriptions of different periods – a kind of pictographic script which conveyed only ideas and concepts, a series of characters resembling an alphabetic script and various forms transitional between the two. On Gran Canaria rock-cut spirals and concentric circles (megalithic petroglyphs) were found in the Barranco de Balos (see A to Z, Agüimes). Only on Tenerife and Gomera has nothing comparable been discovered. The scripts have not so far been deciphered, and it is doubtful whether they ever will be, for souvenir-hunters have broken off much of the rock bearing the inscriptions. It is also uncertain whether the inscriptions were the work of the Canarians themselves or of occasional visitors.

Some handsome pieces of pottery, made without the use of a wheel, have survived from the pre-Hispanic period. Many of them have hollow handles which could also be used as spouts. They are mostly plain and undecorated, but some are patterned with nicks or notches. The forms vary from island to island: thus on La Palma stamped or impressed decoration was used, and on Gran Canaria the decoration was particularly elaborate.

Mention should also be made here of the *pintaderas* – seals

Art

41

Pintaderas: no two the same

in a great variety of patterns, usually made of pottery, rarely of wood. They were presumably used to mark objects with the owner's name. No two pintaderas with the same pattern have so far been found.

There were also figures of idols, presumably used in cult ceremonies, which almost without exception have survived only in fragments. The only one of any artistic quality is the "Idol of Tara", perhaps the most celebrated relic of ancient Canarian culture, which was found on Gran Canaria (now in the Museo Canario in Las Palmas). This clay figure with grotesquely fat limbs is thought to be female, though there are no indications of breasts.

In total, therefore, there are only scanty remnants of ancient Canarian art, all of modest artistic pretensions.

Influences of other cultures

In general the remains of ancient Canarian culture are characterised by archaic simplicity; but there are also elements which appear to belong to a higher cultural level. Thus wheat and barley were ground in a circular hand-mill of a type found in antiquity throughout the Mediterranean region, in which the grain was introduced through a funnel-like opening in the upper stone. Since this piece of relatively advanced technology is out of line with other ancient Canarian remains it is supposed that it was brought to the islands by other peoples. Similarly the rock-cut inscriptions found on the islands may have been left by foreign visitors. It is certainly the case that the Canarians had sporadic contacts with other peoples before the coming of the Spaniards: for example Roman amphoras or fragments of amphoras have been found off the coasts of the islands.

Stone hand-mill, perhaps brought to the Canaries by a foreign visitor

After the Spanish conquest the culture of the ancient Canarians, their language and way of life, fell completely into oblivion. In consequence it was long believed that the conquerors had ruthlessly exterminated the native population. There is no doubt that large numbers of Canarians were enslaved and shipped away from the islands, and that the population was decimated in the fighting with the invaders. Many, however, survived, and anthropological study has revealed the persistence of ancient Canarian characteristics in the present-day population of the Canaries. There must, therefore, have been a very rapid mingling of the two races after the Spanish conquest. The ancient Canarians rapidly became assimilated and adopted the way of life of the Spaniards – not surprisingly, since Spanish culture was so much superior to their own.

Hispanisation of the Canarians

43

Quotations

Homer
"Odyssey"
(8th c. B.C.)

But to thee is assigned, O beloved of Zeus, Menelaus,
Not the destiny of death in Argos, mother of horses;
For the gods will lead thee one day to the end of the earth,
To the Elysian fields, where dark-skinned Rhadamanthys
Dwells, and men are blessed with an ever tranquil life.
There is no snow, no winter storm, no pouring rain;
And there is ever heard the murmur of the softly-breathing West,
Which Ocean sends to bring men gentle coolness.

(Whether the "Elysian fields" described by Homer are to be identified with the Canary Islands is an open question.)

Plutarch
"Life of Sertorius"
(1st–2nd c. A.D.)

There are two islands, separated from one another by a narrow strait, ten thousand stadia from Africa; they are called the Isles of the Blessed. Seldom watered by moderate showers of rain, most commonly by gentle dew-bringing winds, they offer not only a good rich soil to be tilled and planted but also wild fruits sufficient in quantity and flavour to nourish an idle people without work or effort. These islands enjoy a fortunate climate in consequence of the mingling and the barely perceptible change of the seasons; for the north and east winds blowing from our region of the earth are dispersed and die down when they emerge into this expanse of infinite space, and the sea winds from the south and west sometimes bring in moderate rain from the sea but for the most part caress the islands with their gentle breath and make them fertile. And so there has been disseminated even among the barbarians the firm belief that these are the Elysian fields, the dwelling-place of the blessed, of which Homer sang.

Leonardo Torriani
Italian architect
"The Canary Islands and their Inhabitants"
(1590)

The Canarians lived without knowing or feeling illness, at least until they reached the age of 120 or 140. Although their health may also be in part ascribed to the perfection and mildness of the air, yet the main reason must lie in the modest range of foodstuffs, none discordant with another, on which they lived – only barley, boiled, steamed or roast meat, milk and butter, all of which contribute to human health.
From the time the Canarians lived in peace under the rule of their kings they began to build houses and dwellings together and became accustomed to living in towns, giving up their life as tillers of the soil and herdsmen. According to tradition (and as can be gathered from the remains) they had towns of 14,000 hearths, which seems almost impossible. Their streets were narrow and their houses were built in drystone masonry (that is, without mortar or any similar substance), regularly laid and well built, but low. . . . They roofed them with a dense covering of palms, over which, to provide protection from rain, they laid a coating of earth (as is still the practice in Canaria) – for they had no tools with which to practise a nobler form of architecture. For their houses they made small doors with hinges of palm-wood, using saws made from hard, sharp stones held between

two lengths of wood bound closely together, in the manner of a diamond saw. . . . The Canarians had other, older, dwellings built underground . . ., so well and skilfully made that they still seem of eternal duration. In them lived the old, the nobles and the kings, so as to enjoy in winter the warmth withdrawn into the pores of the earth and in summer the coolness which sought refuge there from the hot beams of the sun.

To speake somewhat of these Ilands, being called in old time Insulae Fortunatae, by the meanes of the flourishing thereof, the fruitfullnesse of them doeth surely exceed farre all other that I have heard of: for they make wine better than any in Spaine, they have grapes of such bignesse, that they may bee compared to damsons, and taste inferiour to none: for sugar, suckets, rasins of the Sunne, and many other fruits, abundance: for rosine and rawe silke, there is great store, they want neither corne, pullets, cattell, nor yet wild foule: they have many camels also which being young are eaten of the people for victuals, and being olde, they are used for caryage of necessaries.

Richard Hakluyt
"Principal Navigations . . ."
(1598–1600)

Not without reason is the chief town of Canaria called Las Palmas, for so many groups and groves of palms, with such superb stems, are to be seen nowhere else in the archipelago – not even on the fertile slopes of S. Ursula in the Orotava valley on Tenerife. And here, too, in addition to the Canary palm, there is the date-palm, producing its fruits in abundance.
The outlying part of the town is long and dreary. It leads from Puerto de la Luz to the centre of the city, towards the Guiniguada gorge which divides it into two and opens up a charming view of the sea. The central part of the town is very handsome and of Oriental type, for most of the houses have flat roofs and picturesque *azoteas* (roof-gardens). The almost rainless climate of Las Palmas makes steeply pitched roofs quite unnecessary. A number of bridges span the stony bed of the Guiniguada, and from these there are magnificent views – up into the hills with their profusion of palms and down towards the sea, dotted with sails and traversed by steamers. A little *alameda* runs alongside the river bed. This avenue of palms, combined with the mighty clusters of palms in the gardens to the left, is one of the finest sights the island has to offer; for in addition to the different species of *Phoenix* there are gigantic fruit-bearing specimens of the royal palm and elegant coconut palms with their graceful crowns. All these are present in great abundance and combined into a whole by thickets of tall orange trees. Close to the sea is the fish market, cleaner and daintier than any I have seen: the tables and benches are of marble, the market hall an airy and attractive structure; and nothing can equal the splendour of the fish, brilliant in their metallic glitter of green, sapphire and gold . . .
Crossing the stream, you come into the elegant part of the town, with the cathedral and various public buildings standing round a large and beautifully kept square. The cathedral is an imposing building for such a remote island, not in the vulgar Spanish Jesuit manner but in an unusual Renaissance style. It is fronted by two towers

Hermann Christ
Swiss botanist
"Spring Journey
to the Canaries"
(1886)

45

which taper towards the top. The tall aisles in the interior are separated by columns from which the ribs of the vaulting branch out like the fronds of palms. The view of the nave is blocked by the large retablo which extends across its whole width.

Alexander von Humboldt
German explorer and
naturalist
"From the Orinoco to the
Amazon"
(1889)

On 16th June at 2 o'clock in the afternoon, land at last came in sight, like a small cloud on the horizon. By 5 o'clock, when the sun was already low, the island of Lanzarote lay clearly before us. The current drove us towards the coast more rapidly than we wished. As we approached we saw first the island of Fuerteventura, noted for its large numbers of camels, and soon afterwards the little island of Lobos, in the channel between Fuerteventura and Lanzarote. We spent part of the night on deck. The moon was shining on the volcanic peaks of Lanzarote, whose ash-covered slopes gleamed like silver. The night was marvellously serene and fresh. Although we were not far from the African coast and the boundary of the hot zone, the thermometer showed no more than 18 degrees Celsius. It was as if the luminosity of the sea increased the mass of light in the air. After midnight heavy clouds blew up behind the volcano, now and then obscuring the moon and the handsome constellation of Scorpio. On the shore we could see lights moving hither and thither: probably fishermen preparing to sail.

On the morning of 17th June the horizon was misty and the sky slightly overcast. The mountains of Lanzarote stood out all the more sharply.

In the middle of the archipelago, through which ships sailing to Tenerife seldom pass, we were struck by the resemblance of the coasts to the banks of the Rhine at Bonn.

The island of Lanzarote was formerly known as Titeroigotra. When the Spaniards came here the inhabitants were distinguished from the other Canarians by their higher cultural level. They had houses of dressed stone, while the Guanches on Tenerife lived a troglodytic existence in caves. At that time a curious custom prevailed on Lanzarote. A woman might have several husbands, who alternately acted as head of the household. One man was recognised as head during one orbit of the moon, after which he became a mere servant in the household and another took over his office. It was regrettable that we were unable to learn more about the customs of a people among whom such unusual practices prevailed.

Going by an old Portuguese sailing guide, the captain thought that we were just off an old fort to the north of Teguise, the chief place on Lanzarote. He took the basalt crag for a castle, hoisted the Spanish flag in salute and sent out a boat to enquire of the commandant of the supposed fort if the English were in the offing. We were not a little surprised to learn that the land which we had taken for the coast of Lanzarote was actually the little island of Graciosa and that there was no inhabited place within many miles. . . .

On the morning of 18th June the wind freshened, and we soon lost sight of the little islands of Alegranza, Montaña Clara and Graciosa. Montaña Clara is famed for the beautiful canaries found there. There are also goats, showing that the interior of the island is not so barren as the coast that we had seen.

We live on the slopes of Monte Coello, on the heavy, sharp, stone-crunching Picón and other offshoots of the Pico de Bandama, a nearby volcanic cone which can be seen from Las Palmas and dominates the north-east coast of the island with its regular form. Passengers from the ships which call in for a few hours are almost always brought to this volcano, partly for the magnificence of the view, partly for the thrill of Plutonian terror which the mighty mountain and the adjoining caldera give them. Even if you have been in the Canaries and have seen nothing else, you have at least been on the Pico de Bandama. . . .

On this my first walk I discover that here you move from cultivated land into the wilderness just as quickly and suddenly as in the desert. Even though it bears wheat, the volcanic soil is still wilder than the loneliness of our forests: cultivation is but a transparent veil cast over elemental nature, which emerges nakedly as soon as the planted area ends. Vines reach far up the southern slopes of the hill, the side sheltered from the trade winds: flourishing unpruned among the euphorbias and succulents, standing isolated on the Picón, they look like wild plants to which no one pays any attention. . . .

Standing on the summit, I see the north-east of the island, from the Isletas to the town of Telde, from the sea to the Cumbre; I see the isthmus, the houses of Las Palmas, bathed in a light mist, as if sprayed by water; I see the terraced fields of bananas reaching down towards the town; I see white cubes in the greenery of gardens and plantations. I see all this, but I pass quickly over it: I am drawn to the coast and its fringe of surf, I am drawn to the foam-flecked ocean on which two steamers pitching up from the Tropic are battling ahead. The sea occupies my eyes, uses up my whole visual energy, takes me captive, and I can spare barely a glance for the brown Cumbre, cloud-free though it is. . . .

On the way back I go down into the caldera, which is evidently an older formation than the cone, a kilometre across, 200 metres deep. On its undulating, terraced floor I see fields and a few houses. The slopes on the east side are gentler; on the west side, where rocks emerge, they are steep. Everything is bathed in shades of light brown and grey: no muddy colours and turbid mixtures, but refinement and discreet elegance. I was attracted by the sequestered and insular character of this crater world. With my first steps I left the trade winds and came into stillness. Nothing disturbed me, the clumps of trees which I passed on my way did not stir. But something else was borne in on me with all the might of the trade winds – a wave of volcanic force. I fell into a dream-like daze; from mere joy I was lost to the world, and only came to myself again when I was walking through a thicket of wild olive trees spangled with gay red oleander blossoms and overtopped by palms. A few roofs made of palm fronds, under which cows and goats were standing; fields of maize and tobacco; a stone house, with a woman working in front of it. I turned round: I had walked out of time, far back into the past, and now hastened to return to the present.

Gerhard Nebel
German writer
"Phaeacian Islands:
a Journey to the Canary
Archipelago"
(1954)

Quotations

César Manrique
Spanish artist and architect
"Lanzarote"
(1979)

In the little world of my island of Lanzarote I was able, in the worst possible economic conditions, to carry out my ideas. The result, however, could not have been better: with great passion, great love and full commitment anything can be set in motion.

Lanzarote was born barely fifteen years ago, when it emerged from its anonymity. Before this birth life on the island was hard – very hard. It was a lonely island, from which in bad years many people were compelled to emigrate because they had neither food nor water.

I remember that during my childhood it was still regarded as a shameful thing to be born on Lanzarote. Lanzarote was the Cinderella of the Canaries.

After the great efforts involved in building and in the quest for an individual style for this island branded and burned out by more than three hundred volcanoes, we began to give the island its own original volcanic character, to emphasise its own unique landscape and to pursue the development of a clear, sober, elegant and indigenous architecture. We also began to restore those places which nature had made so incomparably beautiful but which had been disfigured or left to fall into ruin. We have a bad example in the capital of the island, crushed between ruthless blocks of concrete and buried under asphalt and traffic. In this way Lanzarote could become an island of meditation. I say this at the risk of being taken for a Utopian idealist, for a madman.

Lanzarote has thus begun to live out the idea of Utopia, and is now regarded throughout the world as a model, a place where men are trying with all their might to allow nature to recover her original importance. Lanzarote, setting out on the way to economic progress, remembers also its cultural mission. El Almacén, the International Museum of Modern Art and the great auditorium of Los Jameos del Agua are instances of this.

Suggested Itineraries

In this section we suggest a series of itineraries on Gran Canaria. For suggested itineraries on Fuerteventura and Lanzarote see the entries on these islands in the "A to Z" section of this guide.

The description of the tour starts in each case from Maspalomas/Playa del Inglés.

The distances given do not include detours. The general course of the itinerary can be seen from the marginal references. Places which are the subject of a separate entry in the "A to Z" section are printed in **bold** type. Descriptions of other places can be found by reference to the Index.

Route 1: Circuit of the island (c. 190 km/120 miles)

Although Playa del Inglés/Maspalomas is taken as the starting-point of this itinerary, it is of course possible to begin from any place on the route. In general, however, it is better to start with the west of the island, where the roads are not so good and visibility is important. A walk round Las Palmas, on the other hand, is still of interest in the evening, and thereafter it is easy to get back to the tourist resorts in the south of the island on the motorway.

This itinerary, which gives a good general impression of the beauty and interest that Gran Canaria has to offer, can easily be done in a single day, though this will allow only a very short time in any of the places on the route.

Leave **Playa del Inglés** or Maspalomas, going west. In 4 km (2½ miles) the road passes the Pasito Blanco marina, beyond which is the fishing village of **Arguineguín**. The coast here is lined by hotels and apartment blocks, their prospect spoiled by a very conspicuous cement factory at the tip of the promontory. Continuing along the excellent coast road, we come to **Puerto Rico** with its artificially built up sandy beach. The most westerly outpost of the large tourist resorts in the south of Gran Canaria is **Puerto de Mogán**. It is worth having a look round this exclusive colony of holiday apartments (completed only in 1986), which has a marina but lacks an adequate beach. The coast road ends at Puerto de Mogán, and we now turn inland on C 810, which runs north through the fertile Barranco de Mogán. On the slopes of the hills to right and left of the road are little houses with front gardens, occupied during the season by holiday-makers. 8 km (5 miles) from Puerto de Mogán is the little town of **Mogán**. 3 km (2 miles) beyond Mogán a road negotiable by cars goes off on the right to the Embalse de Soria and other artificial lakes. (The road continues to Ayacata, on the route through the centre of the island: Route 2.) In summer, however, it is possible that the lakes may have dried up.

The main road continues north-west, climbing steadily. The vegetation becomes sparser. Some 18 km (11 miles) beyond Mogán a road (the old main road) branches off on the left to a pass, the Degollada de Tasártico. Since the old road

Playa del Inglés/Maspalomas
Arguineguín

Puerto de Mogán

Mogán
Detour to Embalse de Soria and other lakes

Suggested Itineraries

has many bends and offers nothing of special interest, it is preferable to remain on the new and faster road.

Beyond Tocodomán is a more densely settled region, for the plain around **San Nicolás de Tolentino**, with its fertile alluvial soil and abundance of water, is a productive farming area. The mills which pump up the ground-water, worked either by electricity or by wind power, are prominent features of the landscape. Since the water table is steadily sinking, however, many of them are no longer in use. Before the construction of the road San Nicolás de Tolentino's only contact with the outside world was through the little harbour of Puerto de la Aldea. Beyond this point, C 810 runs close to the coast for most of the way.

San Nicolás de Tolentino

Puerto de la Aldea

On this stretch of coast the rocks fall steeply down to the sea, and the road describes a constant succession of bends until, 40 km (25 miles) from San Nicolás de Tolentino, it comes to **Agaete**. The attractive little town of Agaete lies at the mouth of the **Barranco de Agaete,** the most fertile valley on the island. 8 km (5 miles) up the valley is the former spa of Los Berrazales, set amid luxuriant tropical and sub-tropical vegetation (even coffee is grown here).

Agaete
Detour up the Barranco de Agaete

In the centre of Agaete a road goes off to **Puerto de las Nieves,** 1 km (¾ mile) west, from which there is a fine view of the bizarrely shaped rock known as the Dedo de Dios (Finger of God). You can also sample the local seafood in one of the many fish restaurants.

Puerto de las Nieves

We leave Agaete on C 810, going north-east, and in 5 km (3 miles) pass the Cueva de las Cruces (Cave of the Crosses: actually a number of small rock chambers), just off the road to the right.

6 km (4 miles) beyond this is **Gáldar,** a typical little Canarian town. That the site was already occupied in pre-Hispanic times is shown by the La Guancha tumulus. This is most easily reached by taking the road to Sardina, from which a minor road on the right leads to El Agujero. In the immediate neighbourhood of this little hamlet, directly on the sea, is the necropolis of La Guancha (distance there and back 6 km/4 miles).

Gáldar
Detour to
La Guancha tumulus

2 km (1¼ miles) east, now almost joined up with Gáldar, is the little town of **Santa María de Guía** (known for short as Guía), whose economy is centred on banana-growing. Soon after Guía we leave C 810 and continue on the old coast road, with many bends.

Santa María de Guía

Following the signposts, we come to the **Cenobio de Valerón,** one of the most interesting pre-Hispanic sites on the island. From the hill above the caves there is a fantastic view of the stretch of coast known as the Cuesta de Silva, after Diego de Silva, who tried to land here during the Spanish conquest. The old coast road follows a winding course along the hillside to rejoin the excellent modern road at San Felipe. Here the rocks fall less steeply down to the sea than on the west coast, but there are only occasional small bays with beaches of sand or shingle. The fertile land at the mouths of the barrancos is mainly used for banana-growing.

Cenobio de Valerón

From Bañaderos there is a choice of routes.

If you prefer not to include Las Palmas in this circuit of the island you should turn off the coast road at Bañaderos into a road running south, which offers finer scenery and avoids the usually chaotic traffic of the island's capital. This runs

Bañaderos
Alternative route via
Arucas and Tafira

View on the north coast of Gran Canaria

via **Arucas** with its huge neo-Gothic church, Tamaraceite and **Tafira** (where a visit to the Jardín Canario is strongly advised) to Marzagán, from which the motorway will bring you quickly back to the south of the island.

If you continue on the coast road along the north of the island you are soon unpleasantly reminded of the nearness of the city. Along the coast are a series of industrial installations, and just off the road are the makeshift shanties occupied by the poorest of the poor. These impressions, however, are forgotten when you reach the centre of **Las Palmas**, with its many features of interest and its tempting shops.

Las Palmas

South of Las Palmas, in the old district of Vegueta, is the start of the motorway which links the capital with the south of the island. At present it comes to an end at the Aeroclub de Gran Canaria, which can be recognised by the old aircraft set up at the side of the road. From here it is another 7 km (4½ miles) on a very busy road to Playa del Inglés.

Playa del Inglés

Route 2: The interior of the island (*c.* 130 km/80 miles)

This route into the hilly interior of Gran Canaria is undoubtedly the most beautiful on the island. To see the scenery at its best, choose a day when the weather is good. To avoid the clouds which form in the middle of the day it is best to make an early start.

Although the road from Playa del Inglés to San Bartolomé de Tirajana is classed as a secondary road it is well built and presents no difficulties.

Suggested Itineraries

Playa del Inglés/Maspalomas

We leave **Playa del Inglés** by way of the outlying district of San Fernando and follow the signposts north to San Bartolomé de Tirajana. We soon leave the last houses behind us and enter the mountain world, with a succession of magnificent views over the bizarre and barren landscape. The austerity of the country is relieved by small green oases with palms and occasionally orange and lemon trees. In

Arteara

Detour to Embalse de Ayagaures

10 km (6 miles) the road comes to the first village, Arteara. Some 2 km (1¼ miles) beyond Arteara a road (suitable only for a cross-country vehicle) goes off on the left to the Embalse de Ayagaures (30 km/19 miles there and back). A walk to this artificial lake is a good way of getting to know the landscape (not so barren as it appeared at first sight) of this part of the island. From the lake you can find your way back to Playa del Inglés or Maspalomas by way of the tiny hamlet of Alto de la Gorra.

Fataga

The route continues north and soon comes to the first houses of Fataga, a picturesque little place with large numbers of palms.

San Bartolomé de Tirajana

8 km (5 miles) north of Fataga is **San Bartolomé de Tirajana**, the administrative centre of the south of Gran Canaria. Around the little town is an intensively cultivated agricultural region, mainly devoted to fruit-growing. The fruit is used principally in the manufacture of liqueurs and fruit brandies.

Detour to Santa Lucía

You should not miss the chance of a drive from San Bartolomé de Tirajana to **Santa Lucía** with its mosque-like church. Other attractions are the Hao Restaurant and its

The bizarre mountain world of the interior

Fataga: a green oasis

private museum – provided that you do not arrive at the same time as a tourist coach.

10 km (6 miles) beyond San Bartolomé is the tiny settlement of Ayacata.

Ayacata

From here a road diverges to the **Pozo de las Nieves**, the island's highest peak (9 km/5½ miles each way). From the summit, in clear weather, there are fantastic views over the island.

Detour to Pozo de las Nieves

There are also fine views as the road continues towards Tejeda. Just beyond Ayacata, to the right of the road, is the imposing bulk of the **Roque Nublo**. The road then climbs, with numerous bends, to the mountain village of Tejeda, from which it is 7 km (4½ miles) to the **Cruz de Tejeda**, the highest point on the road (1490 m/4889 ft). At the cross and the nearby parador there is almost always a scene of hectic activity.

Tejeda

Soon after the Cruz de Tejeda a road on the left traverses beautiful and almost completely unspoiled country to **Artenara**, which has a cave church and a number of cave dwellings. Beyond this is the idyllic Pinar de Tamadaba, with good walking and tempting picnic spots. From the Cruz de Tejeda to Artenara is 38 km (24 miles) there and back, to the Pinar de Tamadaba 50 km (31 miles) there and back.

Detour to Artenara and Pinar de Tamadaba

From the Cruz de Tejeda the main road runs east to **Vega de San Mateo**, where we turn off into C 814. This passes the Casa Museo de Cho Zacarías and reaches to Valsequillo,

Vega de San Mateo

Valsequillo

53

surrounded by fields in which dry-farming methods are practised. It is particularly beautiful here in December and January, when the almond trees are in blossom. 11 km (7 miles) beyond Valsequillo is the island's second largest town, **Telde**, a busy and rather noisy little town notable particularly for the Iglesia de San Juan Bautista. From here the route continues south on C 812. 4 km (2½ miles) beyond the town a side road goes off to the Cuatro Puertas; it is possible to drive to within 200 m (220 yd) of the cave with its four large entrances. The road then continues to **Ingenio**, where you can buy attractive souvenirs in the Museo de Piedras y Artesanía Canaria, and on to **Agüimes**. Since the other places in the south of the island have nothing particularly new to offer the best plan is to continue south-east from Agüimes to join the motorway at Vecindario/Arinaga. The motorway at present ends at the Aeroclub de Gran Canaria, from which the coast road, often overloaded with traffic, runs past **San Agustín** to Playa del Inglés (27 km/ 17 miles from Agüimes).

Ingenio

Agüimes

San Agustín
Playa del Inglés

Route 3: The north of the island (*c.* 220 km/135 miles)

This route traverses the luxuriant vegetation in the north of Gran Canaria. Since some of the roads have many bends it takes a good deal of time.

The quickest way to reach the north of the island is to take the motorway from **Playa del Inglés** to Las Palmas, leaving it at Mazargán and continuing north-west from there to **Tafira Alta**.
In this area are many handsome villas, set in large gardens, belonging to well-to-do citizens of Gran Canaria. Here a visit should be paid to the Jardín Canario, below Tafira Alta (best reached, when coming from this direction, by way of the Tamaraceite road). From here we continue on C 811 and at Monte Coello take a road on the left to the Pico de Bandama. From the top of the hill there are magnificent views extending as far as Las Palmas and down into the **Caldera de Bandama**. From the foot of the Pico de Bandama a road goes south to the golf course (Campo de Golf) and on to La Atalaya, which is visited on almost every organised tour of the island. 3 km (2 miles) north of La Atalaya we rejoin the main road (C 811), 2 km (1¼ miles) along which is the attractive villa settlement of **Santa Brígida**. The next place of any size is **Vega de San Mateo**, which attracts many visitors on Sundays for the cattle market. In Vega de San Mateo we turn into C 814 for **Teror**, which many consider the prettiest place on Gran Canaria. It has many handsome old houses with beautifully carved balconies. The next place, north of Teror, is **Arucas**, with its huge neo-Gothic church. It is worth climbing the Montaña de Arucas for the sake of the wide views it offers over the surrounding countryside, with banana plantations as far as the eye can reach. Visitors who are tired of the bends in the road and already know the north of the island can return to Las Palmas via Tamaraceite, with fine views of the island's capital and La Isleta.
From Arucas the main route runs west to **Firgas**, which is

Playa del Inglés
Mazargán

Tafira Alta

Monte Coello
Pico de Bandama

La Atalaya

Santa Brígida

Teror

Arucas

Short-cut

Firgas

54

famed for its mineral spring. More interesting than the town itself is the vegetation in the area; thanks to the abundance of water there are flowers and greenery everywhere.

From Firgas we return on the same road to Buenlugar and from there continue west to **Moya**. From Moya the road descends in an endless series of bends to **Santa María de Guía**. If you have not already seen the **Cenobio de Valerón** (see Route 1) you can make a side trip from here. The return to **Las Palmas** is on the new coast road. There is no bypass, so to get on to the motorway to the south it is necessary to drive through the city, which during the rush hour is no particular pleasure.

Thereafter there is a fast run south on the motorway to Playa del Inglés.

Buenlugar
Moya
Santa María de Guía

Las Palmas

Playa del Inglés

Sights from A to Z

Agaete

B2

Altitude: 41 m (135 ft)
Population (district): 4500

Agaete, situated at the foot of Mt Tamadaba in the north-west of Gran Canaria, is the chief town of its district. The inhabitants live almost exclusively by farming. The agricultural produce of the area used to be shipped from Puerto de las Nieves (see entry), only 1 km (½) mile away.
Visitors come here mainly to see the fertile Barranco de Agaete (see entry).

Situation and characteristics

In the centre of this pleasant little town is the modest Iglesia de la Concepción, which has a fine 16th c. Flemish triptych. This is shown only during the Bajada de la Rama (4–7 August), celebrated in Agaete and Puerto de las Nieves, when prayers for rain are addressed to Nuestra Señora de las Nieves (Our Lady of the Snows).

The town

Cueva de las Cruces

5 km (3 miles) from Agaete on the Gáldar road, on the right, is the Cueva de las Cruces (Cave of the Crosses), with a number of adjoining rock chambers which show that the early inhabitants of the Canaries were by no means a primitive people. The inner chambers were adapted to serve the purposes of habitation, and one of the rooms has a fireplace with a chimney opening above it.

Agüimes

C4

Altitude: 286 m (938 ft)
Population (district): 14,000

Agüimes lies roughly half way between Las Palmas and Maspalomas. This must have been a favoured place of settlement in pre-Hispanic times, as is shown by the numerous caves in the surrounding area.
The main source of income of the inhabitants is still farming. The principal crop is tomatoes, but cactuses are also grown on a considerable scale. Thanks to the low lime content of the soil, and to the excellent climate the plants flourish magnificently here, and are usually ready for sale and export only three years after sowing.

Situation and characteristics

◀ *Jardín Canario, Tafira*

The town   Agüimes, with its modest little houses, has little of interest to offer the visitor. Some of the figures of saints in the church are said to be by Luján Pérez.

Lomo de los Letreros

The Lomo de los Letreros ("Ridge of the Inscriptions") is a hill ridge in the Barranco de Balos, a few miles west of Agüimes. It takes its name from the human figures, some of them decidedly bizarre in form, scratched on a 300 m (330 yd) long rock face. Of particular interest is a representation of a boat with a curving prow (no remains of boats dating from the pre-Hispanic period have so far been found in the Canaries). There are also, simple geometric patterns, spirals and circles.

Little of all this will be found by the ordinary visitor without the help of a local guide for the inscriptions are badly weathered, and many later visitors have thought to immortalise themselves by carving their own inscriptions. If, however, you want to try your luck, leave Agüimes on C 815 (the road to Santa Lucía) and in 3 km (2 miles) turn left into a road leading to the hamlet of Los Corralillos (and continuing in a wide curve to the Cruce de Arinaga). 1 km (¾ mile) beyond Los Corralillos take a track on the right (best followed on foot) which runs down into the Barranco de Balos.

Alegranza (Isla de Alegranza)   A10

Situation   The tiny island of Alegranza (area 10 sq. km/3.9 sq. miles) is the most northerly of the Canaries, lying some 20 km (12½ miles) off the north coast of Lanzarote.

Topography   The topography of Alegranza is characterised by cones of tufa and volcanic craters surrounded by short flows of lava. The highest point on the island is Mt Alegranza (289 m/948 ft). The name of Alegranza (= "joy") is said to be an expression of the delight felt by Jean de Béthencourt (see Notable Personalities) on sighting Alegranza, the first island in the archipelago, in 1402: it hardly reflects the superficial aspect of this barren and inhospitable island, now inhabited only by a few fishermen's families. It will appeal to bird-watchers as the home of a number of rare species.

Alegranza can be reached from Lanzarote or Graciosa on a fishing boat.

Arguineguín   D2

Altitude: sea level
Population: 500

Situation and characteristics   Arguineguín lies on the coast of Gran Canaria 12 km (7½ miles) west of the tourist metropolis of Maspalomas/Playa del Inglés. The inhabitants mostly live by fishing. An interesting spectacle for visitors is the fish auction, held when the boats return from sea early in the morning. Tasty fish dishes are served in the village's modest restaurants.

Arguineguín's conspicuous cement factory does not add to its attractions. It has, however, a very small beach, La Playa de Arguineguín, where a number of hotels and apartment blocks have been built.

The village

---

*Artenara   B3

Altitude: 1200 m (3940 ft)
Population (district): 1000

The mountain village of Artenara, in a relatively unspoiled area in the north-west of Gran Canaria, is the highest settlement on the island.
Visitors come to Artenara to see its cave church and to get some impression of the life of its inhabitants, some of whom still live in caves.

Situation and characteristics

At first sight Artenara seems little different from other mountain villages on Gran Canaria. To see the cave church, take the little street which runs up the hill opposite the village church (beside the Casa Consistorial). It ends a few yards from the cave church, which can be recognised by the bell above the entrance. Immediately adjoining the church

The village

The cave church of Artenara . . .   *. . . and its bell*

are a number of cave dwellings, some of which have normal house fronts built on. The inhabitants, however, are not without modern amenities: many of the houses have television aerials.

At the other end of Artenara is a restaurant, the Mesón de la Silla, which is worth a visit even if you are not ready for a meal. The way to it is signposted; the last 100 yards – through a dark tunnel – must be done on foot. From the terrace of the restaurant, huddled against the rock, there is a magnificent view. In the distance can be seen the Roque Bentaiga (1404 m/4607 ft), once a sanctuary and place of sacrifice of the ancient Canarians, and the Roque Nublo (see entry).

Pinar de Tamadaba

The Pinar de Tamadaba can be reached by car only from Artenara on a narrow road (8 km/5 miles) with many bends, but the difficulty of the approach is compensated by the beauty of this pine forest, the finest on Gran Canaria. Many of the tall, slender trees have long lichens hanging from them.

From the mirador (viewpoint, with a picnic area) at the end of the road there is a prospect extending to the coast.

Arucas
B3

Altitude: 250 m (820 ft)
Population (district): 26,000

Situation and
characteristics

The little town of Arucas lies in a fertile valley in the north of Gran Canaria, 17 km (10½ miles) west of Las Palmas. It is the third largest town on the island (after Las Palmas and Telde). The site was occupied in pre-Hispanic times by the Canarian settlement of Arehucas.

The town is surrounded by extensive banana plantations. In the past banana-growing brought it prosperity, but its economy is now very vulnerable to the difficulties of selling Canary bananas in the world market. Sugar-cane, used in the manufacture of rum, is also grown in the area. The rum factory in the town has a daily output of some 50,000 bottles of this powerful spirit.

The town

The most striking feature of the town, visible from a long way off, is the huge Iglesia de San Juan Bautista, built of dark-coloured volcanic stone, which on account of its gigantic size and neo- Gothic style is often referred to as a cathedral. Begun in 1909, it was first used for worship in 1917; the last of its four towers, however, was completed only in the late 1970s.

The Parque Municipal, a small botanic garden, is also worth seeing. In the square in front of the entrance to the park is a monument commemorating the Canarian king Doramas (see below).

Iglesia de San Juan Bautista, Arucas ▶

* Montaña de Arucas

On the north side of the town is the Montaña de Arucas (412 m/1352 ft). A narrow street (signposted) runs up from the church to a large car park from which there are superb panoramic views.

On the summit of the hill the last Canarian king, Doramas, is said to have met the Spanish conqueror, Pedro de Vera, in single combat in 1481. The Spaniard succeeded in killing his opponent only after Doramas had been wounded in a surprise attack.

* Barranco de Agaete   B2

Situation

The Barranco de Agaete, in the north-west of Gran Canaria, extends for 7 km (4½ miles) from the Montaña Gordo (1082 m/3550 ft) to the little town of Agaete.

The Barranco de Agaete is generally agreed to be the most beautiful valley on the island. Its abundance of water fosters a lush growth of vegetation, with plantations of lemons, oranges, mangoes, avocados and other fruits growing amid the palms. The local farmers are particularly proud of their coffee plantations.

Los Berrazales

The road up the Barranco de Agaete ends at the little settlement of Los Berrazales, until a few years ago a much frequented spa to which people came to take the cure in the water of its chalybeate spring. It has now become more profitable to bottle the water and sell it as mineral water. Little is left to recall the former spa, and some of the houses in the village are empty and derelict. Visitors can still, however, find accommodation in the hotel, which is also a lunch-time stop for many coach parties.

* Caldera de Bandama/Pico de Bandama   B4

Situation

The Caldera de Bandama is 10 km (6 miles) south of Las Palmas. The best view of the crater is to be had from the Pico de Bandama (569 m/1867 ft).

Topography

A road runs up to the top of the Pico de Bandama, where there is an observation terrace. Even before reaching the top there are magnificent views into the Caldera de Bandama, a volcanic crater some 1000 m (1100 yd) in diameter and 200 m (650 ft) deep. On the floor of the crater is a farm, surrounded by its fields. This remote and isolated settlement is accessible only by a narrow track running down into the crater. (See Quotations.)

View into the Caldera de Bandama

** Cenobio de Valerón
B3

The Cenobio de Valerón lies above the old coast road a few miles east of Guía. Although this complex of caves is one of Gran Canaria's principal sights, care is necessary to avoid driving past it. There is a small car park off the winding coast road.

The caves, at the top of a flight of 190 steps, are open Monday to Saturday 10 a.m.–1 p.m. and 3–5 p.m.; admission is free.

Situation and opening times

The Cenobio de Valerón is a complex of 298 caves under a natural basalt arch some 30 m (100 ft) wide and 25 m (80 ft) high. The caves, on several levels, are partly natural and partly man-made – hewn by the ancient Canarians from the soft volcanic tufa, which is easy to cut with even the simplest tools. They were formerly closed by wooden doors and linked with one another by passages and flights of steps. One of the higher caves has simple geometric figures scratched on the rock.

Description

The purpose of this large complex of caves has long been a puzzle. Old chroniclers refer to the Cenobio de Valerón as the Convent of the Harimaguadas, sacred virgins who lived here as priestesses. According to another version young girls of marriageable age spent some time in the Cenobio, where they were given a calorie-rich diet so that they might acquire a suitably matronly figure and fit themselves to

Function

63

Cenobio de Valerón

Cenobio de Valerón

become the mothers of large families. Modern research has thrown cold water on the more imaginative theories: the caves may merely have served for the storage of grain.

A chronicler's account

It is known from older accounts that the complex was once even more elaborate than it now is. One of the early chroniclers, Pedro Agustín del Castillo y Ruiz Vergara, describes it as follows:

"When on one occasion I was in the neighbourhood of Guía two of the leading citizens of the town asked me if I should like to see one of the convents of these ancient peoples, situated in a high and steep place above the Barranco de Valerón. The two noblemen took me up to the place, with considerable danger. I confess that the structure filled me with amazement. In a sheer rock face was cut – without sharp iron tools, which were unknown to these early inhabitants, but with no other implement but flakes of flint set into wooden hafts, with which tools, as with axes and picks, they worked timber and felled the strongest trees – a great round arch. Inside the entrance a passage ran inwards, flanked on either side by numbers of cells or chambers, one above the other, provided with windows. On each side of the entrance was a kind of tower, which could be climbed from inside and had window openings looking down into the barranco."

Tagoror

On the rounded hill above the Cenobio lay a *tagoror*, a place of assembly of the ancient Canarians. Remains of stone benches can still be seen.

From the top of the hill there is a good view of the stretch of coast known as the Cuesta de Silva, named after Diego de Silva, who attempted a landing on the north coast of Gran Canaria during the Spanish conquest.

Cruz de Tejeda   B3

The Cruz de Tejeda stands on the highest point of the pass in the centre of Gran Canaria (1490 m/4889 ft). This stone cross is one of the regular stops on coach tours of the island, and there is a bustle of commercial activity aimed at getting the tourists' money. There are stands selling fruit and sweets, and if you are not careful you may find yourself astride a donkey and paying its owner for the privilege.

Situation and characteristics

Although the Parador is only a few yards away from all this activity, in this fine hotel in typical Canaries style you are in a different and more tranquil world. From the terrace (restaurant service) there is a splendid view of fascinating mountain scenery. Miguel de Unamuno (see Notable Personalities) described the scene as "a thunderstorm in stone".

Parador Nacional de Tejeda

Firgas   C3

Altitude: 500 m (1640 ft)
Population (district): 5000

Firgas lies 25 km/15 miles west of Las Palmas in a setting of luxuriant green. There was already a settlement here in the 16th c. The town is famed throughout the Canaries for its mineral water, which is sold on Fuerteventura and Lanzarote as well as Gran Canaria.

Situation and characteristics

Firgas is a little town of modest whitewashed houses on the slopes of a hill. From the town centre a road branches off to the Aguas de Firgas, 5 km (3 miles) away, ending just above the bottling plant.

The town

Fortaleza Grande

See Santa Lucía.

Fuerteventura   A–E3–7

Area: 1731 sq. km (668 sq. miles)
Population: 30,000
Chief place: Puerto del Rosario

Fuerteventura lies between latitude 28° 45' and 28° 2' N and between longitude 14° 31' and 13° 50' W. It is the nearest of the Canary Islands to Africa, only about 100 km (65 miles)

Situation

from Cape Juby. Off the north coast of Fuerteventura is the little island of Lobos (see entry).

Topography

Fuerteventura is the largest of the Canary Islands after Tenerife, extending for more than 110 km (68 miles) from south-west to north-east and measuring 30 km (19 miles) across at its widest point. The centre of the island is occupied by a plateau averaging 300 m (1000 ft) in height, bounded on its east and west sides by low ranges of hills. The main part of the island, known as Maxorata (or Majorata), is linked at its southern end with the Jandía peninsula by the 5 km (3 mile) wide Istmo de la Pared. On the peninsula − part of a huge volcanic crater, the northern rim of which has sunk under the sea − is the island's highest hill, Mt Jandía (807 m/2648 ft).

The visitor's first impression of Fuerteventura is confirmed by a journey into the interior of the island. The hilly terrain has a barren and almost desolate air, the only variety being provided by the colouring of the rocks, which shimmer in various shades of brown and grey. Few visitors would be attracted to the island were it not for its long sandy beaches, still relatively unfrequented − the finest in the whole archipelago, if not in the whole of Europe. Beaches of white sand extend for miles along the north and south coasts, with smaller beaches of black sand in the middle part of the island. It used to be thought that the beaches and dunes of Fuerteventura were created by dust storms from the Sahara, but since the sand consists almost exclusively of carbonates and not of quartzes it must have come from the shallow coastal shelf round the island.

Water supply

The historical records show that in past centuries Fuerteventura had numerous springs; now not one is left. One reason for this is undoubtedly over-use of the island's underground water supplies; all over the island can be seen the windmills which pump up the brackish ground-water. In the heavy showers of rain which occur very occasionally the barrancos are briefly transformed into rushing streams, and the precious liquid is then pounded in the island's three reservoirs; but as a rule the rain is not nearly enough to fill the reservoirs. Much of the water supply of Puerto del Rosario and many villages on Fuerteventura comes from the seawater desalination plant in Las Palmas. Tankers carry the water to the villages, where it is stored in the circular asbestos cisterns to be seen on the roofs of many houses. The larger hotels and tourist settlements have their own water-processing and desalination plants.

The island's name

It is said that the name of Fuerteventura comes from an exclamation by Jean de Béthencourt (see Notable Personalities) during the conquest of the island, "Que fuerte ventura!" ("What a great venture!").

Climate

Fuerteventura's climate shows relatively little variation over the year. In summer it is only slightly warmer than in winter (average annual temperature 22 °C/72 °F), and there is practically no rain. Even in winter there is little rain, and the total annual rainfall is usually no more than 150 mm (6 in). The

Fuerteventura has the most beautiful beaches in the Canaries ▶

Fuerteventura

The barren hills of the interior

humidity of the air ranges between 15 and 55 per cent. The low rainfall does not mean, however, that the island is bathed in perpetual sunshine; there are many days, particularly in winter and more frequently in the north than in the south, when the sky is covered with dense cloud. Sometimes the influence of the Sahara makes itself felt: on the days when the sirocco, a hot dry wind, blows in from North Africa the temperature shoots up 10 °C (18 °F) and visibility may fall to as low as 100 yards, so laden is the air with fine sand.

Vegetation

With a climate like this it is not surprising that Fuerteventura's vegetation is sparse. The hillsides and valleys are bare, with only occasional clusters of palms. Apart from this the commonest plants are spurges, agaves and prickly pears.

Population

Fuerteventura is the most thinly settled island in the archipelago, with only 17 inhabitants to the sq. kilometre (44 to the sq. mile), compared with 27 to the sq. kilometre (70 to the sq. mile) in neighbouring Lanzarote. In the past the unfavourable natural conditions led many of the inhabitants to emigrate, and for centuries the population stagnated: from 10,000 in 1787 it had risen to only 11,500 by 1900. Since 1950, however, there has been a substantial increase in the population, which now stands at about 30,000.

Economy

Economically Fuerteventura long lagged behind the other Canaries. Given the natural conditions, agriculture was possible only on the most modest scale. Maize, wine,

Fuerteventura: as many goats as people?

some kinds of vegetables and figs were produced for local consumption, together with tomatoes, mostly for export. Shortage of water was the predominant problem, and accordingly efforts were made to develop the dry-farming technique known as *enarenado* (see Lanzarote).

Fishing also brings in some income. The island's small fishing fleet at any rate lands enough fish to supply the fish-canning factory in Puerto del Rosario.

Many of the inhabitants live by keeping goats: it is said that there are as many goats as people on Fuerteventura. Since the goats are only rarely kept in enclosed fields visitors will often encounter small herds grazing in open country under the charge of a goatherd. The goats supply meat for local consumption as well as goat's-milk cheese. Between Gran Tarajal and Tuineje is a cheese factory, established in 1985, which sells cheese retail as well as wholesale. For many of the 450 or so islanders who have herds of goats the sale of milk is the only source of income; but great profits are not to be expected, for the she-goats yield only 3–4 litres (5½–7 pints) a day from October to May and 0.5–1 litre (0.9–1.8 pints) in summer.

Tourism

The hopes for the future of the economy, therefore, rest largely on tourism. Here, too, Fuerteventura was a late starter – it is only since the late 1960s that foreigners have been coming to the island in any numbers – but in the 1980s the number of visitors increased substantially. Although the numbers have fallen since 1988 the accommodation continues to increase. At present there are some 25,500 beds available.

One of Fuerteventura's occasional oases of palms

History

When the Spanish conquerors landed on Fuerteventura in the early 15th c. the island was ruled by two kings, their kingdoms separated by a stone wall built across the Istmo de la Pared. In 1405 Jean de Béthencourt succeeded without too much difficulty in bringing the whole island under his control, and established his capital, Betancuria, in the interior. In order to consolidate his rule he settled 200 Spanish and Norman peasants on the newly occupied land. For centuries thereafter Fuerteventura remained a feudal *señorio* ruled by Spanish noble families until 1812.

Until recent times this barren island was much used as a place of exile for critics of the Spanish government in power. Among the exiles who spent some time on Fuerteventura was the writer and philosopher Miguel de Unamuno (see Notable Personalities), who called it an "oasis in the desert of civilisation".

Sights on Fuerteventura

Visitors come to Fuerteventura to enjoy its sun, its beaches and its sea and to practise a variety of sports – the island ranks as Europe's finest wind-surfing area – not to see sights or scenery. If this is accepted, a tour of the island has much of interest to offer.

Since most visitors stay in Jandía, the tour suggested here starts from the south of the island. Those who want to make the circuit in a day should miss out one or two of the places on the route but one place that should not be omitted is Betancuria.

Not so very long ago Morro del Jable was a small fishing village: it is now the island's largest tourist resort. Many large hotels and bungalow complexes have been built to the east of the old village, and this new holiday town, separated from Morro del Jable by a hill, is now known as Jandía.

Morro del Jable/Jandía

The road runs north-east from Morro del Jable, keeping close to the coast for most of the way. Along a stretch of more than 30 km (20 miles) there is a long succession of large and beautiful sandy beaches.

* * Playa de Sotavento de Jandía

40 km (25 miles) up the coast is Tarajalejo, with a small beach of dark-coloured sand, frequented only by small numbers of Spanish visitors.

Tarajalejo

A few miles from the Tarajalejo/Tuineje/Gran Tarajal road junction is the farm of Ponde-Rosa, run by German drop-outs, with large signs advertising the sale of "biological" vegetables. Even if you have no idea of buying vegetables you can visit the community, who are trying out new methods of cultivation and seeking so far as possible to become self-sufficient.

Ponde-Rosa

The little coastal town of Gran Tarajal is almost untouched by tourism. Its harbour is of some economic importance, almost the whole of Fuerteventura's tomato crop being shipped from here. When the choice of the island's capital was under discussion Gran Tarajal ran Puerto del Rosario close.

Gran Tarajal

10 km (6 miles) north of Gran Tarajal is Tuineje. The surrounding area, which has the island's best clay soil, is intensively cultivated; the principal crop is tomatoes. In the 18th c. Tuineje suffered several pirate raids, and the villagers still commemorate, in the annual fiesta of San Miguel on 13 October, an occasion in 1740 when they repelled a raid by English pirates.

Tuineje

Shortly before reaching La Antigua a choice must be made between two alternative routes. One possibility is to take the road which runs east to the sea and continues north up the coast; the other is to take the inland route by way of La Antigua and Casillas del Ánge to Puerto del Rosario.

The first alternative has no features of interest apart from the new development (*urbanización*) known as El Castillo or Caleta de Fustes with its integrated defensive tower. This holiday village, consisting of small bungalows in Moorish-Canarian style, already has something like 1000 beds but is to be still further enlarged. The complex includes a marina. Situated a long way from other settlements or tourist centres, this is a place for a quiet holiday. Compared with the magnificent dune-fringed beaches of Corralejo and Morro del Jable, the beach here is not particularly attractive. Charming features of the resort, however, are the lovingly planned "village square" and the swimming-pool complex around the Castillo de Fustes, a round watch-tower (18th c.) built to provide protection against pirate raids.

El Castillo/Caleta de Fustes

On the second route the next place encountered is the village of La Antigua, which lies in a large and (for

La Antigua

71

An old watch-tower in the holiday village of El Castillo

Fuerteventura) green plain. The white village church contains a much venerated image of the Virgen de la Antigua. At the north end of the village is a handsome round windmill which now houses a restaurant. Beyond it is a State nursery.

La Ampuyenta

5 km (3 miles) north is La Ampuyenta, which has a church dedicated to San Pedro de Alcántara. The church and churchyard are surrounded by a whitewashed wall.

Casillas del Ángel

Much more striking is the church of Casillas del Ángel. This has a bell-cote of dark-coloured stone occupying the whole west front of the church, the rest of which is white. Within the area of the village is an experimental farm run by the island authorities. Here, with luck, you may see some of the dromedaries which are used as working animals on the island's farms.

Puerto del Rosario

15 km (9 miles) from Casillas del Ángel is Puerto del Rosario the chief town of the island (pop. 12,000). It has no features of tourist interest.
Puerto del Rosario became capital of the island at the end of the 19th c., succeeding La Oliva, La Antigua and Betancuria in that role. It was given its present name only in 1957; before that it was known, more prosaically, as Puerto de Cabras (Goats' Harbour). For most of the time it seems almost like a dead town; however, it comes to life in the evening, when the soldiers of the Spanish Foreign Legion fill the streets and patronise the bars and places of entertainment. After the Spanish Sahara gained independence in the mid seventies the 3000 men of the Foreign Legion

Windmill, La Antigua   *Church, Casillas del Ángel*

were stationed here. At first the people of the island were less than enthusiastic about this move, particularly after some legionaries were involved in criminal offences. Since then reasonably good relations have been established between the troops and the islanders – some of whom do quite well financially out of the legionaries.

The Parador Nacional is 4 km (2½ miles) south of Puerto del Rosario on the Playa Blanca. With its walled-in courtyard it has something of the air of a North African caravanserai.

Parador Nacional

The recommended route continues on the coast road which runs north to Corralejo. It soon passes the new Puerto Ventura holiday centre which is being built and then through an extensive area of dunes. The landscape here is constantly in movement, and sometimes the wind forms substantial sand barriers on the road.
Although new hotels and bungalow settlements have been built in and around Corralejo in recent years, this former fishing village has managed to preserve something of its original character. The central feature of the town is a small market square surrounded by restaurants, cafés and shops. From here there is a ferry several times daily to Lanzarote, and a converted fishing boat makes a daily trip to the island of Lobos (see entry).

*Corralejo

From the road which runs south-west from Corralejo a detour can be made (22 km/14 miles there and back) to Cotillo on the west coast. Around this little fishing village there are numbers of secluded bays for bathing and sunbathing, and ideal wind conditions for experienced

Cotillo

wind-surfers. On the outskirts of Cotillo stands the Castillo de Rico Roque, a 17th c. watch-tower.

La Oliva

On the way back from Cotillo, at Lajares (embroidery school), a road goes off on the right to La Oliva, the principal

Casa de los Coroneles

place in the north of the island (pop. 3000). On the east side of the town is the Casa de Los Coroneles (House of the Colonels), an 18th c. mansion, said to have 365 windows and doors, which until the 19th c. was the residence of the commandant of the island. On either side of the plain and undecorated doorway are symmetrically arranged windows and balconies. The house has now rather come down in the world; the surrounding area is mainly populated by goats. The triple-aisled 18th c. parish church is large for the size of the town. The restrained decoration of the interior forms a contrast to the grandiose exterior. The Casa del Capellán, near the church, is now half ruined but preserves interesting Aztec motifs on the façade.

Montaña Quemada

2 km (1¼ miles) south of the village of Tindaya, at the Montaña Quemada, is a memorial to Miguel de Unamuno (see Notable Personalities), a huge monument set in front of a dazzlingly white wall.

Embalse de los Molinos

Farther south, a few miles south-west of Tefia (from the village, follow the signposts to "Los Molinos"), lies the Embalse de los Molinos, an artificial lake formed by a dam 102 m (335 ft) long and 42 m (138 ft) high on the Barranco de los Molinos. A system of canals leads water from the lake to the nearby agricultural settlement area of Las Parcellas. The lake is seldom well filled; often it is only a metre deep for a distance of only a few metres.

*Betancuria

The most beautiful place on the island is undoubtedly Betancuria, founded by Jean de Béthencourt in 1405, which until 1834 was the island's capital. Nowadays the village, surrounded by gardens and cultivated fields, has a population of some 500.
The central feature of the village is the Iglesia de Santa María (founded by Béthencourt), which was destroyed by pirates in 1539, rebuilt in the first half of the 17th c. and

thoroughly restored in 1986. The church contains a number of notable works of art. The gilded high altar dates from the second half of the 17th c. The statue of Santa Catalina is dated to the late 15th c., making it one of the oldest pieces of woodcarving in the Canaries. In the sacristy is preserved the Pendón de la Conquista (Banner of the Conquest), which is believed to be the 15th c. original. The sacristy itself has a fine Mudéjar-style wooden ceiling.

In a house immediately adjoining the church is the Museo de Arte Sacro with four rooms containing various objects of religious art.

In the main street of the town is the Museo Arqueológico (Archaeological Museum), with two old cannon outside the entrance. The exhibits include domestic equipment, tools and weapons of past centuries, a document recording the Spanish conquest of the island and relics of the ancient Canarians, including a mummified body.

Near the south end of the town are the remains of a Franciscan friary (Ruinas del Convento) in which San Diego de Alcalá, a native of Seville, is said to have lived.

5 km (3 miles) south-west of Betancuria is the village of Vega de Río de las Palmas, situated in an area which, in comparison with other parts of Fuerteventura, is well supplied with water. Here a few palms grow and tomatoes and other vegetables are cultivated.

Vega de Río de las Palmas

The Ermita de Nuestra Señora de la Peña, near the Embalse de las Peñitas (an artificial lake which is usually dry), is the scene of an annual pilgrimage on the first Saturday in September. The chapel, which now houses the alabaster statue

Betancuria

of the Virgen de la Peña, is built over a cave in which the Virgin is said to have appeared to San Diego de Alcalá in the 16th c.

Pájara

8 km (5 miles) from Vega de Río de las Palmas on a winding road is Pájara, with the two-aisled Iglesia de la Virgen de la Regla (1645–87). The doorway of the church has decorations with Aztec motifs like those on the Casa del Capellán in La Oliva, which are not found on any of the other islands in the Canaries.

The return journey from Pájara to Morro del Jable is by way of Cortijo de Chilegua and Matas Blancas (c. 60 km/37 miles).

Cofete

With a vehicle suitable for cross-country work it is possible to drive on an unsurfaced road from Morro del Jable to Cofete. The trip will appeal only to those who want to spend some time on Cofete's lonely and beautiful beach. To reach it, take the road to the Punta de Jandía and in a few miles turn into a road on the right, indicated by an inscription on a stone in lieu of a signpost. The most important establishment in Cofete is the bar. A few hundred yards from this is the Villa Winter, a handsome mansion built by a German engineer of that name on a site granted to him by General Franco for services in the development of Spain. Since Winter had close relations with the Nazi régime in Germany there were wild rumours, during and after the Second World War, that the villa was a centre of German espionage. After the war it was believed to be a staging point for prominent Nazis on the way to South America. The former owners of the house are now long since dead.

*Gáldar   B2/3

Altitude: 143 m (469 ft)
Population (district): 19,000

Situation and characteristics

Gáldar, situated at the foot of the Pico de Gáldar (434 m/1424 ft) in the north-west of Gran Canaria, is easily reached from Las Palmas (28 km/17 miles) on the excellent new coast road. It is now gradually joining up with Santa María de Guía (see entry). From whichever direction you approach the town there is no doubt about the basis of its economy: it is surrounded by extensive banana plantations. Visitors come to Gáldar to see its remains of the pre-Hispanic period and buy the local produce in the market.

History

There was a settlement here before the Spanish conquest. Gáldar was the seat of one of the two kings of Gran Canaria, whose "palace" is believed to have been on the site now occupied by the Iglesia de Santiago de los Caballeros. According to the early chroniclers it was a rectangular building with handsome beams of Canary pine. The Spanish conquerors re-used this excellent timber, leaving no trace of the residence of the *guanarteme*, as the Canarian king was called.
When Juan Rejón set about the conquest of the island in 1478 the local ruler was Tenesor Semidan, who held sway

View from Gáldar across to Tenerife

over the north-western half of Gran Canaria. Having taken refuge in a cave with some of his followers, he was captured by the Spaniards and forcibly baptised, after which he sided with the conquerors and persuaded his people to surrender and accept Christianity. A few hundred yards east of Gáldar's main square is a monument to him, unveiled by King Juan Carlos in 1986.

Since most visitors make only a brief stop at Gáldar on a tour of the island, the town has preserved much of its original character. Its life centres on the shady Plaza de Santiago, and in the surrounding streets are numbers of small shops and workshops. A centre of attraction for local people is the market in Calle Capitán Quesada (which branches off the Guía–Agaete road).

The town

Sights

In the tree-shaded Plaza de Santiago, in the centre of Gáldar, is the church of Santiago de los Caballeros, completed in 1872 after a building period of almost 70 years. The green font immediately to the right of the entrance, now framed in wood, is believed to have been brought from Andalusia at the end of the 15th c. and used in the forcible baptism of the Canarians. The church also contains a number of statues of saints attributed to Luján Pérez (including "The Incarnation of Christ" and "Mary of the Rosary").

Iglesia de Santiago de los Caballeros

Also in the square, a few yards from the church, is the Ayuntamiento (Town Hall). During the opening hours of

Ayuntamiento

the municipal offices (mornings only) a fine specimen of a dragon tree can be seen in the courtyard. It was planted in 1719, and there is now barely room in the patio for its branches and its roots.

**Cueva Pintada
More restoration work took
place in the mid-1980s

The Cueva Pintada (Painted Cave) is to the right of the road (when coming from Guía) at the south-west end of the town (signposted). The cave was discovered in 1873, but was not restored until 1970–74.

It is not known what the function of the cave was, whether a place of burial, a dwelling or a place of sacrifice.

The Cueva Pintada is of particular interest for its rock paintings, for nothing comparable to them has been found on any of the neighbouring islands. On the walls of the cave, which measures 5 m by 4.5 (16½ ft by 15) and is 3 m (10 ft) high, are painted geometric figures – squares, triangles and concentric circles. Similar figures have been found in mainland Spain. This lends support to the theory that the ancient Canarians were related to European peoples (see Early Inhabitants, Origin).

Open: Tue.–Sun. 10 a.m.–1 p.m. and 4 p.m.–6 p.m.

Sardina (Puerto de Sardina)

A short distance beyond the south-west end of Gáldar a road (6 km/4 miles) goes off on the right to Sardina, a little fishing village which attracts many Canarians at weekends to its modest sandy bays and its excellent fish restaurants.

Faro de Sardinia

From the Faro de Sardina, a lighthouse 3 km (2 miles) from the village, there is a charming view of the coast.

La Guancha

La Guancha is reached from Gáldar by taking the Sardina road and almost at once turning right into a side road signposted to the La Guancha necropolis at El Agujero, on the coast. This is a circular structure of stones laid without mortar, with two round burial chambers in the centre surrounded by many smaller rectangular chambers. The chambers were originally roofed with stone slabs. When the necropolis was excavated in 1935 thirty mummies dating from the late 11th c. were found. It seems likely that this was the burial place of Canarian nobles; the two larger circular chambers may have belonged to the royal family.

* Graciosa   B10/11

Area: 27 sq. km (10.4 sq. miles)
Population: 500
Chief place: Caleta del Sebo

Situation

The island of Graciosa lies off the northern tip of Lanzarote, separated from it by a strait only 1500 m (1650 yd) wide at its

La Guancha necropolis

narrowest point. There are regular day trips to the island from Órzola on Lanzarote in a converted fishing boat; only a few individual visitors spend longer on Graciosa.

Graciosa is an island of low volcanic cones (the highest of which is Agujas Grande, 266 m/873 ft) and sandy plains (drift sand consisting largely of carbonates). Palaeontological investigation has revealed large numbers of land snail shells, the presence of which is difficult to explain in present-day climatic conditions.
The great attraction of Graciosa lies in its "dream beaches", the finest of which are to the west of Caleta del Sebo and on the north-west coast (Playa de las Conchas).

Topography

The little settlement of Caleta del Sebo in the south-east of Graciosa is occupied only by a few fishermen and their families. There are a number of *pensiones* providing accommodation for holidaymakers (*c.* 30 beds).
In the north-east of the island is another tiny settlement, Pedro Barba.

Caleta del Sebo

Montaña Clara

The island of Montaña Clara, off the north-west coast of Graciosa, has an area of only 1 sq. km (250 acres). In the centre of the island a volcano (256 m/840 ft) high rises out of a barren expanse of lava.

Guía

See Santa María de Guía

Ingenio   C4

Altitude: 339 m (1112 ft)
Population (district): 21,000

Situation and characteristics

The village of Ingenio lies 30 km (19 miles) south of Las Palmas, near the Aeropuerto de Gando. Its name (Spanish, "sugar-mill") is an indication of its main source of income in earlier times: in the 16th and 17th c. in particular it prospered by the production of sugar and later of rum. The main crop nowadays is tomatoes.

The village

With its little white houses and simple parish church, Ingenio is a very typical Canarian village.

Museo de Piedras y Artesanía Canaria

Visitors come to Ingenio not so much for the village itself as for the Museo de Piedras y Artesanía Canaria (Museum of Rocks and Canarian Handicrafts) at the north end of the village. Outside the museum a number of items of old agricultural equipment are displayed. The museum is mainly a showroom for the sale of Canarian handicrafts;

The Museum of Rocks and Canarian Handicrafts, Ingenio

attached to it is an embroidery school (which can be visited). The collection of rocks has little to offer the non-expert, and many of the exhibits are inadequately labelled or not labelled at all.
The museum is open daily from 9 a.m. to 6 p.m.; admission free.

La Atalaya

See Santa Brígida

La Guancha

See Gáldar

Lanzarote

B–D8–11

Area: 795 sq. km (307 sq. miles)
Population: 54,000
Chief place: Arrecife

Lanzarote, the most easterly of the Canaries, lies between latitude 29° 13' and 28° 50' N and between longitude 13° 55' and 13° 24' W, 115 km (71 miles) from the coast of Africa. Off its northern tip are the small islands of Graciosa (see entry), Montaña Clara and Alegranza (see entry).

Situation

The island's greatest length from north to south is 60 km (37 miles), its greatest breadth from east to west 20 km (12½ miles). There is more evidence of volcanic activity on Lanzarote than on any other island in the Canaries: it has something like 300 volcanic cones, varying in height but mostly between 400 and 600 m (1300 and 2000 ft). The highest peak is the Peñas del Chache (671 m/2202 ft). At the north end of the island the hills fall steeply down to the strait between Lanzarote and Graciosa, El Río; at the south end they merge gradually into the coastal plain of El Rubicón. The interior of the island is a lunar landscape. Between 1730 and 1736 and again in 1824 the western part of the island was shaken by numerous eruptions, centred in the area now known as the Montañas del Fuego (Parque Nacional de Timanfaya), and some 20 per cent of the island's area was buried under a layer of lava between 6 and 10 m (20 and 35 ft) deep. Volcanic activity has not yet entirely sub-sided, as is shown by the high temperatures recorded immediately below the earth's surface in the Montañas del Fuego.
Although on the west side of the island the coast falls steeply down to the sea, some of the flat sandy beaches on the east and south coasts (see Practical Information, Beaches) offer ideal conditions for bathing.

Topography

Lanzarote

Water supply

Water supply has always been a problem on Lanzarote, which has neither springs nor much ground-water. Rainwater was collected in cisterns, but after a long period of drought – and sometimes there is no rain on Lanzarote for a year at a time – many people were compelled to leave the island. In more recent times water has had to be brought in by tanker to meet a crisis of this kind. With the arrival of mass tourism other solutions had to be found, and since 1968 seawater desalination plants have alleviated the shortage of water. This ensures that the tourist centres are adequately provided for; but the local people still have to put up with occasional rationing of supplies.

The island's name

Lanzarote probably owes its name to a Genoese, Lancelot Maloisel (Lanzarotto Malocello), who landed on the island in 1312 and held it until 1330. An alternative explanation suggests that when Jean de Béthencourt heard about the taking of the island in 1402 he broke his lance in delight (Spanish *lanza rota* = "broken lance"). However, since the island was already known by its present name in the 14th c. this can be no more than a good story.

Climate

Like the other islands in the Canaries, Lanzarote is subject to the influence of the north-eastern trade winds, with the strongest winds in spring and summer. Since the air currents come up against no hills of sufficient height on Lanzarote, however, the trade winds do not cause much cloud formation or rainfall on the island. The average annual precipitation, therefore, is extraordinarily low at under 200 mm (8 in). The rain falls almost exclusively in autumn and winter. The average annual temperature is about 22 °C (72 °F).

Vegetation

As a result of its low rainfall Lanzarote has a very sparse vegetation cover and no woodland at all. In a few sheltered spots there are groves of palms; otherwise the native vegetation consists predominantly of tamarisks and euphorbias. Prickly pears, an imported species, have spread widely over the island.

Population

In contrast to the smaller islands in the western Canaries, Lanzarote has shown a steady increase in population. From barely 18,000 in 1900 the population rose to almost 30,000 in 1950, and it is now about 54,000. More than half the island's inhabitants live in Arrecife (30,000 inhabitants), where the population continues on a rising trend, while in the smaller places on the island it is either static or actually falling.

Economy

In spite of the fact that it hardly ever rains on Lanzarote and that the island's resources of ground-water are very limited, agriculture makes a major contribution to the economy. Special methods of cultivation adapted to the terrain have been developed. To allow the plants to reach the soil under the surface layer of lava the farmers dig out funnel-shaped holes about a metre (40 inches) in diameter, and in these depressions, sheltered from the wind, vines and vegetables are successfully grown. To ensure sufficient moisture in the

By dromedary into the Montañas del Fuego ▶

soil a dry-farming technique known as *enarenado* (from *enarenar*, to sprinkle with sand) is adopted. The soil is covered with a 30 cm (12 in) thick layer of lapilli (small pieces of lava about the size of a walnut), which, being highly porous, store up the moisture which falls at night in the form of dew. They also have the quality of warming up during the day and cooling quickly at night, which increases condensation from the layers of air near the ground. The layer of lapilli is renewed every 30 years or so. This method of cultivation is practised on a large scale around La Geria (see entry). A similar process is applied with sand. A belt of sand 3–5 km (2–3 miles) wide, known as El Jable, runs across the island from north to south; and since sand, like lapilli, is good at storing up moisture even this region of dunes can be developed for agriculture.

Lanzarote's most important agricultural product is wine, of which it is the largest exporter in the Canaries. In addition potatoes, tomatoes, maize, onions and other vegetables are grown.

A major contribution to the economy is also made by the rearing of the cochineal insect, which is used in the production of a red colouring substance. The insect feeds on the prickly pear, and in the mid 19th c. fields of prickly pear began to be planted to provide a food supply for these tiny parasites. The colouring substance is contained in the larvae of the cochineal insect. After mating the females lay their eggs over a period of about 14 days, covering the prickly pears with a whitish gossamer web. At "harvest" time the larvae are stripped off the plant, killed in hot water

Dry farming at La Geria

and dried. In the 19th c. this was a very profitable business, but with the development of aniline dyes the economic importance of the cochineal insect declined. While in the past cochineal was used in the dyeing of textiles it is now used only in the manufacture of lipsticks and for colouring aperitifs, aerated waters, sweets and specimens for microscopy. This natural product is also used for the dyeing of valuable Persian carpets.

A contribution is also made by the winning of salt from seawater. There are a number of saltworks on the island, the largest being the Salinas de Janubio. A small proportion of the salt is processed to produce table salt; most of it is used in the salting of fish products.

The island's coastal waters – particularly between Lanzarote and Africa – are well stocked with fish. Not surprisingly, therefore, Arrecife is the base of the largest fishing fleet in the Canaries. Catches are amply sufficient to supply the fish-canning plant in Las Palmas.

Prickly pear with cochineal insects

Compared with the neighbouring islands of Tenerife and Gran Canaria mass tourism came to Lanzarote relatively late. In 1968 there were only 10,000 visitors to the island, but thereafter the figure rose rapidly – to 25,000 in 1970, 80,000 in 1975 and well over 600,000 in 1987. Most of the visitors come from West Germany, Britain, Scandinavia and mainland Spain. In 1989 there was a drastic reduction in the number of holidaymakers on both Gran Canaria and

Salinas de Janubio

Lanzarote, but 80% of Lanzarote's business still comes from tourism. Most of the visitors come from West Germany, Britain, Scandinavia and mainland Spain.

History

It is only from the early 14th c. that we have any clear picture of the history of Lanzarote. In 1312 Lancelot Maloisel, a Genoese, landed on the island which bears his name, and thereafter held it until 1330. At first contacts between the European incomers and the original population of the island remained sporadic. A century later, however, the situation changed. In 1402 Gadifer de la Salle and Jean de Béthencourt (see Notable Personalities) achieved a quick conquest of the island, and it then became the base for further conquests in the Canaries. Subsequently Lanzarote passed into the hands of various noble families, until in 1478 the Spanish Crown reasserted sovereignty over the island. Until 1837 Lanzarote was a *señorio*, a feudal holding which was granted by the Crown to nobles and high ecclesiastics.

As a protection against pirate raids the Spaniards established the administrative centre of Lanzarote in the interior of the island, and until 1852 this function was held by Teguise. Nevertheless Lanzarote continued to be harried by pirates, and, particularly in the 16th c., many of its inhabitants were carried off into slavery.

The volcanic eruptions between 1730 and 1736 were catastrophic for Lanzarote. The most fertile parts of the island were devastated, and the continuing eruptions led many of the inhabitants to emigrate.

Visitors to Lanzarote cannot help noticing that there is less to offend the eye here than on other islands in the Canaries. No electricity pylons are to be seen; the telephone lines are carried underground; attractive hotel buildings and well laid out viewpoints fit beautifully into the landscape; no large advertising signs are allowed. For all this Lanzarote has mainly to thank one man, the artist and architect César Manrique (see Notable Personalities), who has been fighting for years to prevent the over-commercialisation of the island.

Arrecife

General

The island's capital and port, on the east coast, owes its name (*arrecife* = "reef") to the many small ridges of rock off the coast. Arrecife has been the administrative centre of the island only since 1852. The town's sheltered harbour promoted its rapid growth, and more than half the island's population (*c.* 30,000) now live in Arrecife. During the rush hour the traffic in the town tends to get into a hopeless snarl-up.
Arrecife is not only important as the base of the Canarian deep-sea fisheries, with several canning factories: it is also the centre of Lanzarote's commercial life. So far the town

has remained largely untouched by tourism, with only a single large hotel complex in Avenida Mancomunidad – perhaps because the town's beaches are not particularly inviting. Altogether Arrecife is an attractive little town with a beautifully planted seafront promenade, a handsome town centre and two restored fortresses.

On a tiny offshore island, linked with the town centre by the Puente de las Bolas (Bridge of the Balls), is the Castillo de San Gabriel, a fortress built in 1590 by the Italian architect Leonardo Torriani to protect the east coast of Lanzarote from pirate raids. It now houses a small historical museum; open Mon.–Fri. 8 a.m.–1 p.m.

Castillo de San Gabriel
(at present being restored)

The Castillo de San José, at the north end of the town, was built in 1779 on the orders of King Carlos III. Although also designed to serve a military function, it was probably built mainly to provide work for the impoverished rural population. In fact it was never used as a fortress: until 1890 it served as a munitions store, and thereafter it lay empty for many years.

*Castillo de San José/
Museo Internacional de
Arte Contemporáneo

In the 1960s, at the instigation of César Manrique, the building was restored, and with financial support from the government Manrique was able to buy pictures by artists of international reputation. The fortress now houses the Museo Internacional de Arte Contemporáneo (International Museum of Contemporary Art), which possesses works by Picasso, Miró, Tapiez, Vela, Albers and other artists, as well as some of César Manrique's own paintings.

Castillo de San José

The restrained decoration of the rooms in the museum (designed by Manrique) makes a fitting background for the pictures. A curving staircase leads down to a lower floor, with a restaurant from the long window front of which there is a view of the open sea.
The museum is open daily from 11 a.m. to 9 p.m.; admission free.

Iglesia de San Ginés

In the centre of Arrecife is the Iglesia de San Ginés, which is dedicated to the island's patron saint. The church, otherwise quite plain, has a handsome colonial-style façade.

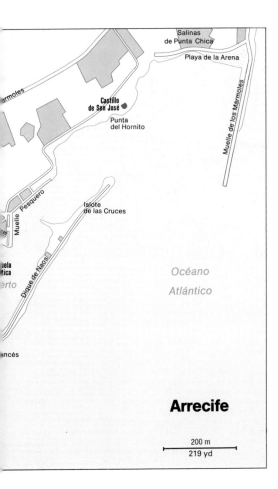

Salinas
de Punta Chica

Playa de la Arena

Muelle de los Marmoles

Castillo
de San José

Punta
del Hornito

armoles

Muelle Pesquero

Islote
de las Cruces

Dique de Naos

uela
tica

rto

ncés

Océano

Atlántico

Arrecife

200 m
219 yd

**Parque Nacional de Timanfaya/Montañas del Fuego

The Montañas del Fuego (Mountains of Fire), at the western
end of Lanzarote, are the central feature of the Parque
Nacional de Timanfaya (Timanfaya National Park), which
covers an area of 5107 hectares (20 sq. miles). The National
Park, established in 1974, is unquestionably Lanzarote's
principal tourist attraction. Visitors can drive to the Islote de
Hilario and from there join a guided party on a drive round
the Ruta de los Volcanes. Alternatively, they can explore the

89

Parque Nacional de Timanfaya

area on a dromedary; the starting-point is on the road from Yaiza to the Montañas del Fuego.

Opening times
The National Park is open daily from 9 a.m. to 4.45 p.m.

Origin
Until the 18th c. the Montañas del Fuego area was one of the most fertile parts of Lanzarote, with numerous small settlements; then between 1730 and 1736 there were repeated volcanic eruptions which caused immense devastation. An eye-witness, the village priest of Yaiza, wrote: "On 1st September, between 9 and 10 in the evening, the earth suddenly opened near Timanfaya, two miles from Yaiza. In the first night a gigantic hill rose out of the earth, and the summit of the hill discharged flames, which blazed without cease for 19 days." But this was only the beginning, and there were a whole series of further eruptions until 1736. The people of the island were compelled to abandon their homes and seek refuge on Gran Canaria. After a long pause there were further eruptions in 1824, since when the volcano has been quiescent. As a result of the eruptions in the 18th and 19th c. some 20 per cent of the island's total area was covered with a layer of lava 6–10 m (20–35 ft) thick.

Topography
The area is now a bizarre lunar landscape. Great expanses of lava extend over the whole of the National Park, shimmering in black, grey, yellowish and red hues. Out of the lava flows rise numerous volcanic cones and craters, the highest of which is Timanfaya (510 m/1673 ft).

Flora
The inhospitable volcanic terrain is only gradually acquiring a scanty cover of vegetation. The most tenacious plants are the lichens, of which there are a dozen species. After them come succulents, such as *Aeonium lancerotense* Praeger, and euphorbias (*Euphorbia balsamifera* Ait., *E. obtusifolia*

Poir.). Also common is *Aulaga majorera* (*Zollikoferia spinosa* Boiss.), which the guides at the Islote de Hilario set on fire for the benefit of tourists. A curious feature on the coast, where the lava flows have formed natural rock bridges, is the growth of reeds (*Juncus acutus* L.) in regular rows on the porous soil with its store of water.

The only vertebrates in this area are reptiles, the commonest and most interesting of which is an endemic species of lizard, *Lacerta atlantica*.

Fauna

The road into the Montañas del Fuego ends at the Islote de Hilario. At this crater, where the highest soil temperatures in the whole region are recorded, is a restaurant designed by César Manrique, the Restaurante del Diablo. Since only a few metres under the surface the temperature is about 400 °C (750 °F), only fireproof materials were used in its construction. The circumstances of the area have been turned to advantage, and the restaurant grills its steaks solely with the aid of this natural heat. Visitors are given other demonstrations showing how hot the soil is. A National Park employee pours a jugful of water into an iron pipe in the ground, and a few seconds later the water shoots out again in a shower of steam; then he puts a handful of brushwood in a crevice in the ground, and the twigs quickly catch fire.

Islote de Hilario

The most interesting of the natural phenomena in the National Park can be seen in the course of a 14 km (8½ mile)

Ruta de los Volcanes

In the Parque Nacional De Timanfaya

drive round the Ruta de los Volcanes (Volcano Route). A coach leaves Islote de Hilario at regular intervals and travels along the Volcano Route (cost is included in the charge for entry to the park). The main stops on the route are the viewpoint on the Montaña Rajada, the Valle de la Tranquilidad, with older volcanic cones covered with a layer of more recent ash, and the view of the Caldera de los Cuervos, one of the largest craters.

Other sights on Lanzarote

The other features of interest on the island are described in the form of a round trip starting from Arrecife. If you want to see all the sights described at least two days will be required. If you are only on a day trip to Lanzarote you should confine yourself to the principal sights (La Geria, Montañas del Fuego, Teguise, Cueva de los Verdes, Jameos del Agua).

Aeropuerto de Arrecife

Few airports in the world qualify as tourist sights, but Lanzarote's airport undoubtedly does. From the outside it is not particularly impressive, but the interior is very different. Designed by César Manrique and decorated entirely in white and green, it has something of the aspect of a garden; it succeeds in being not only functional but also aesthetically attractive.

Puerto del Carmen

From the airport the coast road runs south-west and comes in a few miles to the tourist resort of Puerto del Carmen. Until quite recently a tiny fishing village, this has developed into the island's principal tourist centre. Hotels and apartment blocks, rows of shops and restaurants extend for miles along the main road. More than two-thirds of all visitors to Lanzarote stay in Puerto del Carmen, attracted by the beautiful beaches in the area, the most popular of which is the Playa Blanca.

*La Geria

Inland from Puerto del Carmen, 8 km (5 miles) north-west, is the La Geria plateau. The volcanic eruptions of the 18th and 19th c. covered the area with a thick layer of ash, and special methods of cultivating the soil had to be devised (see Economy, p. 25). The funnel-shaped depressions in the ground and the contrast between the dark volcanic ash and the green of the vines give the landscape an exotic aspect. The Museum of Modern Art in New York described this method of cultivation as an example of engineering without engineers.

Salinas de Janubio

The route continues by way of Uga and Yaiza, two villages of white cube-shaped houses, to the Salinas de Janubio on the west coast, the largest saltworks on the island. Here seawater is pumped into small basins and left for a month or so. The water has then evaporated, leaving a layer of salt, which is formed into small heaps to dry. The Salinas de Janubio produce some 30 tonnes of salt a day in summer and 15 tonnes a day in winter; the total annual output is about 10,000 tonnes.

El Golfo

El Golfo, 9 km (5½ miles) north of the Salinas de Janubio, is a semicircular crater now filled by a small lake. While the east side of the lake is still bounded by the 20 m (65 ft) high

The crater lake of El Golfo

wall of the crater, the west side of the crater has been eroded by the sea. The curious greenish colouring of the lake is due to a species of alga in the water. Evaporation and the seeping in of seawater have given the lake an unusually high salt content – higher, it is said, than the Dead Sea.

15 km (9 miles) south of El Golfo is Playa Blanca, a small fishing village around which increasing numbers of apartment blocks and holiday homes are being built (ferry from here to Fuerteventura). The beaches of Playa Blanca itself are not particularly inviting; much more beautiful are the Playa de Papagayo, Playa de las Coloradas and Playa de Mujeres, a few miles east.
The road to these beaches passes the Castillo de las Coloradas, sometimes called the Torre del Aguila (Eagle's Tower). The fort which was built here by the Spanish conquerors at the beginning of the 15th c. as a base for the conquest of Fuerteventura was destroyed by pirates in 1749 and replaced by the present watch-tower.

Playa Blanca

To continue the circuit of the island the best plan is to return to Yaiza. A few miles beyond this, on the left of the road leading to the Montañas del Fuego, is the dromedary station. Here you can join a party on dromedaries to see the Mountains of Fire. Soon afterwards the entrance to the Parque Nacional de Timanfaya (see p. 89) is passed.

8 km (5 miles) farther on is the village of Tinajo, which has a church with a sundial of 1881.

Tinajo

Continuing south-east from Tinajo by way of Tiagua and

Lanzarote

Monumento al Campesino

Tao, we come, just after Mozaga, to the Monumento al Campesino, a dazzlingly white piece of sculpture, 15 m (50 ft) high, erected by César Manrique (see Notable Personalities) in honour of the peasants of Lanzarote, who win a harvest from the soil with so much labour.

The Casa del Campesino, beside the monument, houses a restaurant and a showroom for the sale of souvenirs. Since water is a precious commodity on Lanzarote, the building is designed so that rainwater from the roof is conveyed directly into cisterns.

* *Teguise

Teguise, the old capital of the island, is 8 km (5 miles) north-east of Mozaga. The town was founded by Maciot de Béthencourt and named after one of the last native kings. Although situated inland, it frequently suffered from pirate raids: the name of the Callejón de la Sangre ("Lane of Blood") recalls these violent days. Teguise was the birthplace of the writer José Clavijo y Fajardo (see Notable Personalities). It is famed for making the best *timples* in the Canaries. These small stringed instruments, still handmade in small workshops in traditional fashion, are produced in different sizes and different qualities.

The central feature of Teguise is the market square; the market held here every Sunday has become a big tourist attraction. However, few of the stall-holders appear to be local farmers or artists; the bulk are foreigners offering fashion jewellery and bric-a-brac as well as home-baked bread and jams.

One side of the market-place is bordered by the Palacio de Spinola, built in the 18th c. by a Genoese merchant named Vicente Spinola. After extensive restoration work directed by César Manrique it is now used for conferences and as a residence for distinguished people. The whole house – living and reception rooms, kitchen and bedrooms, all beautifully decorated and furnished – is open to the public (daily 9 a.m. to 4 p.m.). Some of the rooms are used for periodic special exhibitions.

Opposite the palace is the Iglesia de San Miguel. The oldest parts of the church date from the 15th c., but it underwent much alteration in later centuries.

Other relics of Teguise's past – it was the first episcopal see in the Canaries – are two monastic houses. The half-ruined Convento de Santo Domingo, at the south end of the town, dates from the 18th c.; the Convento de San Francisco, at present being renovated, goes back to the 16th c.

On a volcanic hill above Teguise is the Castillo de Guanapay or Castillo de Santa Bárbara, founded by Lancelot Maloisel in the 14th c. and enlarged and strengthened by Leonardo Torriani at the end of the 16th c. It is planned to instal a small military museum in the castle.

Haría

15 km (9 miles) north-east of Teguise is Haría. There is a fine view of the town from the Mirador de Haría, looking down into the fertile valley with its scatter of little white houses and the innumerable palms which have earned Haría the name of the "town of a thousand palms".

*Mirador del Rio

At the northern tip of Lanzarote is the Mirador del Río, designed by César Manrique and opened in 1973. The restaurant and observation platform are completely integrated

Palacio de Spínola, Teguise

In the courtyard of the Palacio de Spínola   *Iglesia de San Miguel*

Haría

into a crag which falls steeply down to the sea. From here there is a fantastic view of the small islands of Graciosa (see entry), Montaña Clara and Alegranza (see entry). The interior of the restaurant is deliberately restrained so as to avoid any distraction from the magnificent setting.

*Cueva de los Verdes

The Cueva de los Verdes, 10 km (6 miles) south-east of the Mirador del Río, was also developed by César Manrique into a tourist attraction. Of this 6100 m (6700 yd) long cave system 2000 m (2200 yd) have lighting and are accessible to visitors. In the past this underground labyrinth served as a refuge for the local people in times of volcanic activity and during raids by pirates or other attackers. One of the lower chambers is now a concert hall with seating for an audience of 1000.
The cave is open daily from 11 a.m. to 6 p.m.

*Jameos del Agua

The Jameos del Agua, another show cave 2 km (1¼ miles) east, belongs to the same cave system as the Cueva de los Verdes. Here, too, the influence of César Manrique can be seen. Steps lead down to a restaurant partly built into the cave, the name of which comes from the small salt-water lake it contains, formed by the seeping in of sea-water. In the lake lives a blind white crab (*Munidopsis polymorpha*), which is usually found only at a depth of over 3000 m (10,000 ft). At the end of the cave, on a higher level, is an attractive garden, beautifully laid out by Manrique, with numerous tropical and subtropical plants and a dazzlingly white swimming pool. The complex also includes a concert hall with seating for 800 in the crater of an extinct volcano.

Jameos del Agua

With its excellent acoustics and its fascinating spectrum of colours, this makes an impressive setting for concerts and performances of folk singing and dancing.
The Jameos del Agua is open daily from 11 a.m. to 6.45 p.m.; on Tuesdays, Fridays and Saturdays it is also open in the evening (double admission charge after 7 p.m.).

Around Mala and Guatiza are huge fields of prickly pears, on which the cochineal insect is reared (see Economy, p. 25).
In March 1990 the Jardin de Cactus was opened in Guatiza. This cactus garden was designed by César Manrique and covers an area of 10,000 sq. m (12,000 sq. yds).
Going from Guatiza on to Tahiche and thence in the direction of Arrecife, on the right-hand side of the road out of Tahiche you will see the former workshop and dwelling of César Manrique (Taro de Tahiche).
Now that the artist has retired to Haria the "Volcano House" is to be turned into a museum.

Mala/Guatiza

Near Manrique's house a little road branches off left to the holiday development of Costa Teguise, where the influence of César Manrique is everywhere to be seen. The holiday accommodation and facilities here are in typical Lanzarote style, largely in tones of green and white. The central feature is a luxury hotel, Las Salinas, with a unique swimming-pool complex and an overwhelming profusion of greenery. Every conceivable kind of sport can be practised at Costa Teguise, which includes among its amenities a boating marina and a golf course.

Costa Teguise

Las Palmas (Las Palmas de Gran Canaria)   B4

Altitude: 0–210 m (0–689 ft)
Population: 366,000

Situation and
characteristics

Las Palmas de Gran Canaria, chief town of the province of
that name and of the island of Gran Canaria, occupies the
north-eastern tip of Gran Canaria. The city extends along
the coast for a distance of some 14 km (9 miles) and is
bounded on the landward side by the foothills of the island's
central massif. The peninsula of La Isleta (the "Islet") was
incorporated in the city within the present century. La Isleta
was in fact originally an islet, but was joined to Gran Canaria
by a spit of land which built up over the centuries.

With its population of 366,000 Las Palmas is by far the
largest city in the Canaries and the eighth largest in Spain. It
has long been a major centre of industry, commerce and
communications, much of its importance being due to its
harbour (Puerto de la Luz). Its favourable situation at the
intersection of shipping routes between Europe, Africa and
South America enabled it to become one of the world's
largest Atlantic ports.

The many thousands of visitors who come to Las Palmas
from all over the world, whether as seamen or as tourists,
have given it something of an international atmosphere. It
has some 200 hotels; but many foreign visitors prefer to see
the sights of this rather noisy and hectically busy city in a
day trip and spend the rest of their holiday in the south of the
island with its more reliable sunshine.

▼ Las Palmas and the Isleta

The town was founded on 24 June 1478 by Juan Rejón, who made it his base for the conquest of Gran Canaria for the Spanish Crown. Situated in an area where there were then large numbers of palms, it was named Ciudad Real de las Palmas (Royal City of the Palms). The first notable event in its history was the visit of Columbus (see Notable Personalities), who stayed in Las Palmas on his first and fourth Atlantic voyages, residing in the house which was later named after him, the Casa de Colón. During the late 15th and the 16th centuries the town was involved in a struggle for survival, having repeatedly to beat off attacks by English, French and Portuguese forces. Its severest trial was in 1599, when a Dutch force of 10,000 men under van der Doez tried to take the town.

During the 17th and 18th c. Las Palmas prospered, and many handsome buildings were erected in the Vegueta quarter, some of which have survived into our day. The town's rapid rise, however, began only after the construction of the harbour at the end of the 19th c. From 16,000 in 1860 the population rose to almost 50,000 by 1900. Las Palmas expanded in all directions, the old quarter of Vegueta and Puerto de la Luz coalesced, and new residential districts grew up above the coastal zone. When tourism began to develop in the 1950s there was a regular building boom along the Playa de las Canteras, and new hotels mushroomed.

Las Palmas has been the island's capital since 1820, and when the Canaries were divided into two provinces in 1927 it was promoted to become capital of the eastern province of Las Palmas de Gran Canaria.

Las Palmas

The various quarters of Las Palmas have very different characters, and the city has no real centre. The main tourist area is round the Parque de Santa Catalina and along the Playa de las Canteras, with the circular tower block of the Hotel Los Bardinos as its principal landmark.

Immediately east of the Parque de Santa Catalina is the harbour district, extending on to La Isleta.

Most of the tourist sights are in Vegueta, the oldest part of the town. The central feature of this quarter is the Plaza de Santa Ana, the scene of popular fiestas and processions. In the surrounding streets are many fine old houses with handsome façades, elaborately decorated wooden balconies and quiet patios.

The city's best residential district is the Ciudad Jardín (Garden City) round the Parque Doramas. In the quiet side streets of this area are sumptuous villas set in luxuriant gardens. The owners are evidently fearful of burglars: almost every house has an alarm system and grilles over the windows, and anyone taking photographs is regarded with suspicion.

The main shopping street is Avenida de Mesa y López, with numerous department stores and large shops. Smaller shops are to be found in the pedestrian zone in Calle de Triana, which runs through the district of that name.

In sharp contrast to the exclusive Ciudad Jardín and the commercial districts with their well-stocked shops are the slum areas which extend along the road to Gáldar and the west side of La Isleta, where the poorest classes of the population live in shanties of wood and corrugated iron. It is not surprising, in these conditions, that crime has taken on horrendous proportions in Las Palmas.

In the following section the features of interest in Las Palmas are described from north to south. Although it is about 5½ kilometres (3½ miles) from the Castillo de la Luz, on the harbour, to the Plaza de Santa Ana sightseeing is best done on foot, in view of the chaotic traffic conditions that regularly prevail in the city.

Puerto de la Luz

Work began on the construction of Puerto de la Luz at the end of the 19th c. under the direction of an engineer named Juan de León y Castillo. In terms of freight handled (6.9 million tonnes) it takes sixth place among Spanish ports, but in terms of shipping movements it does better than this, with some 14,000 ships putting in every year. The Muelle de Santa Catalina, near the Parque de Santa Catalina, is used by the car and passenger ferries between the islands in the Canaries and also by services to mainland Spain. Some fishing boats also anchor here, but the real fishing harbour is the one enclosed by the Muelle Pesquero. The Muelle de la Luz is used mainly by cargo vessels. The outermost pier is the Dique del Generalísimo, where the large tankers and cruise ships moor.

Near the Muelle Pesquero, in Calle de Juan Rejón, stands the Castillo de la Luz, built in the 16th c. to protect the town against pirate raids. This massive fort, which is surrounded

Castillo de la Luz

by gardens, is to become a museum; it is at present used for
occasional special exhibitions.
(Open Monday to Friday 11 a.m.–2 p.m. and 5–9 p.m.,
Saturdays 11 a.m.–2 p.m.)

*Playa de las Canteras

The Playa de las Canteras, one of the longest city beaches in
the world, extends for some 2.6 km (1½ miles) on the north-
west side of Las Palmas. Long barrier reefs lying off the
coast protect it from the strong surf and ensure safe bathing. Considering their situation, both the beach and the sea
are remarkably clean. The beach becomes crowded at
weekends, which thousands of Spaniards like to spend by
the sea.
Along the Playa de las Canteras extends the Paseo de las
Canteras, a seafront promenade with innumerable hotels,
cafés, restaurants and shops.

Parque de Santa Catalina

The Parque de Santa Catalina lies in the centre of the tourist
quarter of Las Palmas. In this shady square are a number of
cafés, and hawkers of many nationalities offer their wares.
In the Casa del Turismo visitors can get leaflets and information.

Las Palmas
de Gran Canaria

600 m
656 yd

*Parque Doramas

In the centre of the Ciudad Jardín with its trim villas lies the Parque Doramas, named after the last Canarian king of the eastern part of the island. The park displays typical Canarian flora, including a number of fine specimens of dragon trees. An attraction for children is the mini-zoo at the north end of the park.

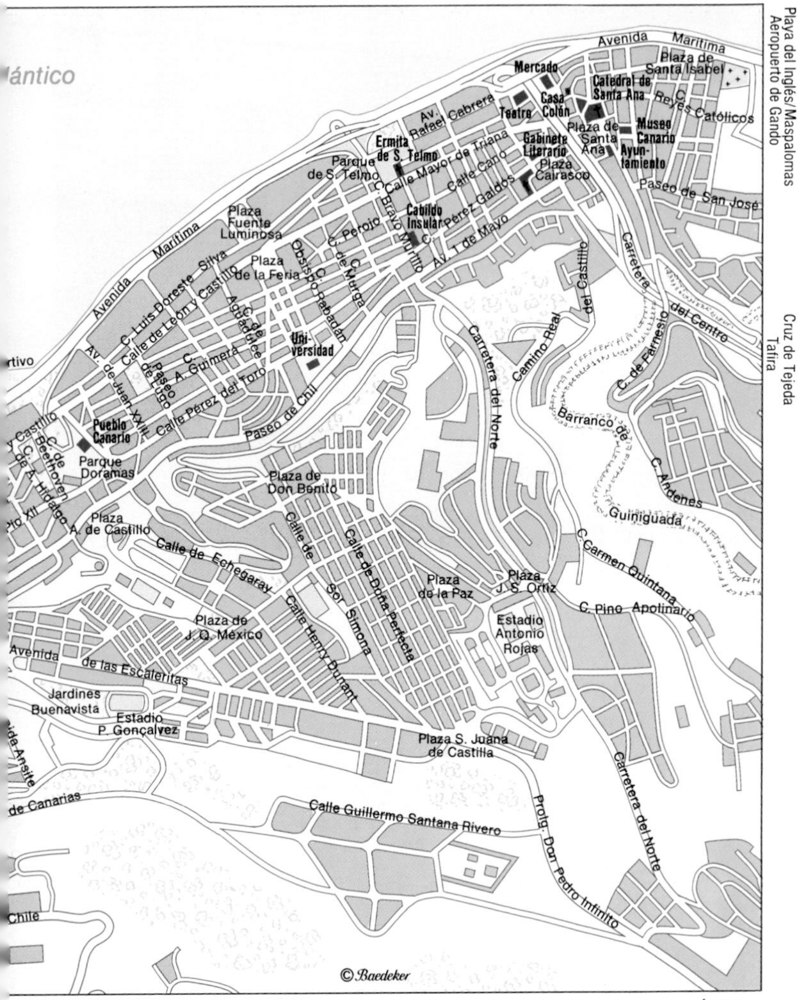

The luxurious Hotel Santa Catalina (photograph, p. 145) fits inobtrusively into the landscape of the park. Built in 1953, it is in the style known as Canarian Baroque.

The Pueblo Canario (Canarian Village), on the edge of the Parque Doramas, was established in 1939 as an example of traditional Canarian architecture, based on the plans and watercolours of Néstor de la Torre (see below).

Pueblo Canario

103

The Museo Néstor in the Pueblo Canario

In the courtyard of the group of houses are souvenir shops, the entrance to the Museo Néstor and a café. Here you feel far from the noise of the city – the stillness being interrupted only by the performances of folk singing and dancing which are regularly given here.

Museo Néstor

In the Pueblo Canario, opposite the café, is the Museo Néstor, opened in 1956, which contains works by the Canarian painter Néstor Martín Fernández de la Torre (1887–1938: see Notable Personalities), together with various items of furniture from the artist's studio. Many of Néstor's most notable paintings show the influence of Symbolism. In Room 1 the "Wedding Poem" and a self-portrait of the artist are among the most important works. The pictures of typical Canarian buildings in Room 2, painted between 1934 and 1938, were intended as models for new buildings to meet the needs of the tourist trade. The paintings in Room 3, on the theme "Atlantic", date from 1913 to 1924. Room 4 contains portraits, Room 5 drawings done between 1934 and 1938, Room 6 sketches (1913) of sets for Mozart's "Don Giovanni", Room 7 sketches of stage sets and costumes for various ballet productions, Room 8 plant studies. The pictures in Room 9 are on the theme "Earth". Room 10 displays drawings and sketches for major works from all the different periods of the artist's career.
(Open Monday, Tuesday, Thursday and Friday 10 a.m.–noon and 4–7 p.m., Saturday 10 a.m.–noon, Sunday 10.30 a.m.–1.30 p.m.).

The Altavista viewpoint is reached by going west from the
Parque Doramas, crossing the broad Paseo de Chil and
continuing west past a monument to the engineer Juan de
León y Castillo. From the viewpoint there is a superb prospect over Las Palmas and the sea.

Altavista viewpoint

Triana

Triana is the oldest shopping and commercial district in Las
Palmas. Most of the shops are in the Calle Mayor de Triana,
now a pedestrian precinct paved with flagstones.

The Calle Mayor de Triana runs past the Parque de San
Telmo, in which is the Ermita de San Telmo. This little
chapel dedicated to the patron saint of fishermen has a fine
coffered ceiling in Mudéjar style. The chapel contains many
ex-votos, mainly from seamen rescued from peril on the
sea.

Ermita de San Telmo

At No. 6 Calle Cano, a street parallel to the Calle Mayor de
Triana, stands the house in which the writer Benito Pérez
Galdós (see Notable Personalities) was born and spent his
early years. The house, now a museum, contains an interesting collection of Pérez Galdós's works and many personal mementoes and relics of the writer.
(Open Monday to Saturday 9 a.m.–1 p.m.; admission free.)

Museo de Pérez Galdós

The Gabinete Literario (Literary Cabinet) in Plaza de Cairasco, in the south-west of the Triana quarter, is an imposing building with fine stucco decoration in the interior. It is
now used for exhibitions and lectures.

Gabinete Literario

Adjoining Plaza de Cairasco is Plaza de San Francisco, with
the 17th c. church of San Francisco, which has a number of
statues in wood by Luján Pérez.

Iglesia de San Francisco

Near the south end of the Calle Mayor de Triana is the Teatro
de Pérez Galdós, built in 1919. The foyer has murals by the
Canarian painter Néstor de la Torre.

Teatro de Pérez Galdós

The Mercado de las Palmas, near the theatre, is the oldest of
the city's four market halls.

Mercado de las Palmas

*Catedral de Santa Ana

The Catedral de Santa Ana is in the Vegueta quarter, the
oldest part of Las Palmas. Both the exterior and interior of
the church reflect the fact that it was built over many centuries. Construction began in 1497, but work stopped in
1570, though the part of the church which had been completed by then, in Gothic style, could be used for worship.
The neo-classical west front, designed by Luján Pérez, was
completed in the late 18th and early 19th c.
The Cathedral has double aisles flanking the nave. The
Gothic ribbed vaulting is borne on slender columns. The
rich furnishings include a Baroque high altar and various

105

Catedral de Santa Ana

Plaza de Santa Ana

Treasures in the Museo Diocesano de Arte Sacro

works by Luján Pérez. In the crypt is a monument to the
Canarian poet and historian José de Viera y Clavijo (d. 1813).
The Cathedral can be visited only during services (Monday
to Friday 8–10.30 a.m.; Saturday 7–10.30 a.m. and 7–9 p.m.;
Sundays and public holidays 7 a.m.-1.30 p.m. and 6.30–
8 p.m.) or through the Museo Diocesano de Arte Sacro.
The stairs up one of the towers are at present being reno-
vated. From the top there is a fine view of Las Palmas.

The Museo Diocesano de Arte Sacro (Diocesan Museum of   Museo Diocesano de Arte
Sacred Art) is housed in one of the aisles of the Cathedral.   Sacro
Among its treasures are statues of saints (including some
by Luján Pérez), a small collection of pictures, including
works by 16th c. Flemish painters and 17th and 18th c.
Canarian artists, and numerous gold and silver liturgical
objects.
From the Museum there is access to the quiet courtyard of
the Cathedral and to the Cathedral itself.
(Open daily 9 a.m.–1 p.m.)

The west front of the Cathedral looks on to the Plaza de   Plaza de Santa Ana
Santa Ana. In the square are a number of bronze figures of
dogs, from which the island is supposed to have taken its
name (see Facts and Figures, Origin of name). Opposite the
Cathedral is the Ayuntamiento (Town Hall). On the north
side of the square is the Palacio Episcopal (Bishop's Palace).

**Casa de Colón

Beyond the east end of the Cathedral is the handsome Casa
de Colón (House of Columbus). The house, which was
rebuilt in 1777 in typical Canarian style, was once the residence of the governor of the island. Columbus is believed to
have lived here during his brief stay on Gran Canaria (see
Notable Personalities). The building now houses a museum
(entrance in Calle Colón) with exhibits on "Columbus and
his Time" and pictures of the 17th to 19th c. (mostly on loan
from the Prado in Madrid).
There are two beautiful patios, one of them containing a
Gothic fountain.
(Open Monday to Friday 9.30 a.m.–1.30 p.m., Saturday
9 a.m.–1 p.m.)
The Casa de Colón also houses the Museum of Fine Art
(entrance in Plaza del Pilar Nuevo), with works by contemporary Canarian painters.

100 km (110 yd) east of the Casa de Colón is the Ermita   Ermita de San Antonio
de San Antonio Abad, in which Columbus prayed before   Abad
setting out on his voyage into the unknown. The chapel,
originally 15th c., was rebuilt in the 18th c.

**Museo Canario

The Museo Canario, the finest museum in the archipelago,
is at Calle Doctor Verneau 2, to the south of the Plaza de
Santa Ana.
Originally opened in 1800, the Museo Canario was

Casa de Colón
House of Columbus

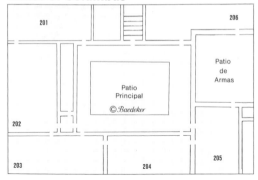

UPPER FLOOR

201 16th and 17th c. pictures
202 17th and 18th c. pictures and sculpture
203 18th and 19th c. pictures
204 South American art
205 Gran Canaria:
    relief model of island, etc.
206 Las Palmas:
    model of town in 1685;
    ground plan of Castillo de la Luz

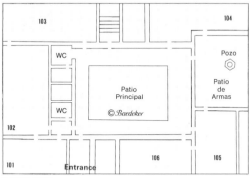

GROUND FLOOR

101 Voyages of discovery:
    maps illustrating Columbus's view of the world and the stages of
    discovery of the New World
102 Columbus and his voyages:
    models of the "Pinta", "Niña" and "Santa María", etc.
103 The world of the conquistadors
104 Cartography
105 Archaeological finds from Colombia
106 Archaeological finds from Mexico

Casa de Colón

completely rebuilt in the middle of the 1980s. Since its reopening it has proved to be a modern museum laid out on pleasingly instructive lines. It provides an excellent insight into the culture and way of life of the early inhabitants of the Canary Islands. The archaeological finds and anthropological exhibits are complemented by models and diagrams; in one room, for example, is a reproduction of a living-room with everyday objects and various ceramic utensils used by the ancients. Also on view are more than 1000 skulls (the rarest include some on which brain-operations have been carried out), numerous skeletons and some mummies. The reconstruction of the necropolis of La Guancha (see Gáldar) gives a good impression of the way the early inhabitants buried their dead.

Among the numerous ceramics, items of jewellery and household utensils, the stone hand-mills and *pintaderas* (terracotta seals) (see photographs on p. 42) are of particular interest. The exact purpose of the latter is still not known for certain. Since no two pintaderas have been found with the same design it is assumed that they were used to stamp objects with a mark of ownership. The best-known ancient Canarian work of art is the Idol of Tara, a pottery figure with grotesquely fattened limbs which appears to be female, though there are no indications of breasts.

Attached to the museum is a reference library of 40,000 volumes. The books are either connected with the Canaries in some way or by Canarian authors.

(Open Monday to Friday 10 a.m.–1 p.m. and 3–7.30 p.m.; Saturday 10 a.m.–noon; library Monday to Friday 4–7.30 p.m.)

Ermita de San Antonio Abad

In the centre of Las Palmas

*Lobos (Isla de los Lobos)   A7/8

Situation	The island of Lobos (area 6 sq. km/2.3 sq. miles) lies in the Bocaina, a channel only about 30 m (100 ft) deep between Fuerteventura and Lanzarote and which is notorious for its strong currents. The nearest points of Lobos and Fuerteventura are only 2 km (1¼ miles) apart.

A converted fishing boat sails daily from Corralejo on Fuerteventura to Lobos, returning in the late afternoon; the crossing takes half an hour.

Topography

Essentially the island consists of a recent volcano (Lobos, 127 m/417 ft), with smaller subsidiary craters, and an almost unspoiled area of dunes. Although this is a nature reserve it is regularly used for military training, during which the island is declared a closed area.

There is good bathing on the Playa de la Arena (east coast) and Playa del Sobrado (west coast).

The barren terrain of Lobos affords a living only to a few families of fishermen. Accommodation for visitors is of the most modest description.

Lomo de los Letreros

See Agüimes

Maspalomas

See Playa del Inglés/Maspalomas

Mogán   C2

Altitude: 250 m (820 ft)
Population (district): 8000

Until quite recently Mogán, situated at the upper end of the   Situation and
Barranco de Mogán in the south-west of Gran Canaria, was   characteristics
a remote mountain village, but within the last few years
it has begun to be discovered by tourists, and the village
and its fertile valley have also attracted adherents of the
"alternative" culture.

Mogán is a long straggling village caught between high   The village
rock walls. Thanks to the abundance of water in the bar-
ranco the houses have luxuriant gardens. Some of them
have signs advertising rooms to let.

Montaña Clara

See Graciosa

Moya   B3

Altitude: 488 m (1601 ft)
Population (district): 7500

Moya, the chief place in the district of the same name, lies   Situation and
30 km/20 miles west of Las Palmas in the foothills of   characteristics
Gran Canaria's central massif. It was the birthplace of the
Canarian poet Tomás Morales (1885–1921).

The central feature of the little town is the shady plaza, with   The town
the church of El Pilar. Close by is the house in which Tomás
Morales was born. It now houses a library, and is also used
for public functions of various kinds.

Pico de Bandama

See Caldera de Bandama/Pico de Bandama

Pinar de Tamadaba

See Artenara

Playa del Inglés/Maspalomas D3

Altitude: sea level

Situation and characteristics

The two hotel towns of Playa del Inglés and Maspalomas in the south of Gran Canaria have now coalesced to form by far the largest tourist centre on the island. The south-western part of the resort is Maspalomas, the north-eastern part Playa del Inglés, with Calle Alfereces Provisionales marking the approximate boundary between the two. This huge new development is in stark contrast to the Oasis de Maspalomas round the lighthouse (the Faro de Maspalomas). A number of luxury hotels and apartment blocks surrounded by palms give the resort an attractive air.

Playa del Inglés and Maspalomas owe their popularity to the broad sandy beach which extends for 6 km (4 miles) to the east of the Faro de Maspalomas.

Origin

Towards the end of the 1950s the local landowner, Don Alejandro del Castillo, Conde de la Vega Grande, had the idea of creating a tourist resort on this otherwise valueless site. At that time there was not even a fishing village in the area, and there was only a narrow asphalted country road into the southern part of the island. This was soon to change. The Count, who can trace his ancestry back to Maciot de Béthencourt (see History), founded a number of building and civil engineering companies and secured a monopoly of the water supply. By the end of the sixties his investment began to bear fruit, as visitors flocked in huge

Dunas de Maspalomas

numbers to the new hotels and apartments. Playa del Inglés and the adjoining developments now have some 120,000 hotel beds.

It is evident at first sight that Maspalomas and Playa del Inglés have not grown up naturally. The town, consisting solely of large hotels, bungalow colonies and apartment blocks, huge shopping centres and countless restaurants, cafés and discos, might have been built anywhere in the world. Depending on the season, the wide four-lane highways and oversize roundabouts are barely adequate to cope with the traffic or are almost deserted. In the side streets of Maspalomas and Playa del Inglés it is difficult to know where you are, so similar to one another are the various hotel complexes set amid luxuriant gardens.

The resort

**Dunas de Maspalomas

Some people like Playa del Inglés/Maspalomas, others do not; but there is no disagreement about the beauty and fascination of the dunes and beaches to the south and west of the resort. Like the dunes on Lanzarote and Fuerteventura, the Dunas de Maspalomas were not formed by wind-borne sand from the Sahara, as used to be thought; the sand, consisting almost exclusively of carbonates, is of marine origin. The dunes are up to 10 m (35 ft) high in places.
An area of 328 hectares (810 acres) has been scheduled as a nature reserve, but in spite of this the ecological balance of the area is endangered, and the rare flora and fauna adapted to the arid conditions have already been decimated. The authorities have therefore taken steps to ensure that there is no further building in this unique area of dunes, and a hotel complex already under construction at the Faro de Maspalomas was demolished in 1989.

Holiday World

Holiday World, the first amusement park in the Canaries, lies on the west side of Maspalomas. This area of 14,000 sq. m (3½ acres) appeals to young and old, local people and visitors alike, with its wide range of attractions – a 27 m (90 ft) high Ferris wheel, a roller-coaster, a variety of roundabouts, dodgem cars and even a Mississippi steamer sailing on an artificial lake.
In view of the shortage of water in this part of Gran Canaria it is remarkable how much greenery the park contains. Tall palms, cactuses, agaves and flowering plants, plantings of Canarian flora in a natural setting and a number of fountains combine to form an agreeable setting for the park's various attractions.

Open Mon.–Fri.
5 p.m.–12.30 a.m.;
Sat., Sun. and pub. hol.
3 p.m.–12.30 a.m.

**Palmitos Parque

Palmitos Parque, 10 km (6 miles) north of Maspalomas, is reached on a road which leaves the west end of the resort and runs north into the hills. The park, in a valley flanked by

Open daily 9.30 a.m.–
7 p.m.

high hills, was established in the early 1970s and now has an area of over 200,000 sq. m (50 acres). It contains some 50 species of palms and innumerable cactuses and agaves. The fauna includes gibbons and 230 species of birds. The pond in the centre of the park is home to numbers of ducks and swans, while flamingoes and peacocks stalk about on the surrounding lawns. The principal attractions, however, are the numerous parrots. Like the Loro Parque on Tenerife, the Palmitos Parque does not merely keep the parrots for show: it also breeds them. One of the most popular attractions in the park is a 20-minute show, put on eight times a day, in which fifteen gaudily coloured macaws go through their tricks. Although weather conditions are not always favourable – at this height (400 m/1300 ft) it can become distinctly cold at night – it is planned to extend the park still further.

There are regular bus services to Palmitos Parque from

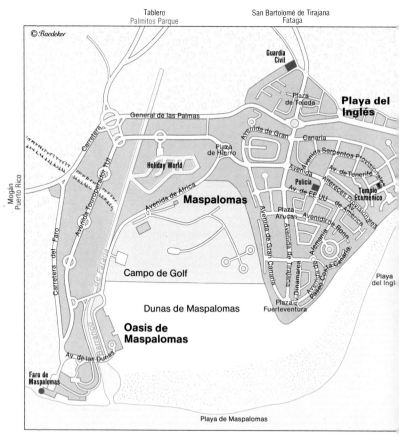

Maspalomas (bus station near golf course; buses every 30 minutes), San Agustín and Puerto Rico.

* Pozo (Pico) de las Nieves   C3

Gran Canaria's highest hill, the Pozo de las Nieves ("Well of Snow") or Pico de las Nieves (1949 m/6395 ft), occupies the centre of the island. The summit – which, as its name indicates, is sometimes covered with snow in winter – can be reached on either of two roads, one starting from the Cruz de Tejeda, the other from the village of Ayacata. From the top, provided that it is not shrouded in the dense clouds brought by the trade winds, there are superb views of the surrounding hills.

Situation and topography

Costa Sur de Gran Canaria
Maspalomas · Playa del Inglés · San Agustín

700 m
766 yd

Pozo (Pico) de las Nieves

Palmitos Parque

Dedo de Dios, Puerto de las Nieves

Puerto de las Nieves   B2

Altitude: sea level

Puerto de las Nieves, 2 km (1¼ miles) west of Agaete (see
entry) on the north-west coast of Gran Canaria, was in the
past a port of some consequence. The agricultural produce
of the Agaete area was shipped from here, and vessels
sailing between Las Palmas (Gran Canaria) and Santa Cruz
(Tenerife) used to call in. Now the short pier is used only by
a few fishing boats.
Visitors come to Puerto de las Nieves to see the Dedo de
Dios (below) or to have a meal in one of the excellent fish
restaurants.

Situation and
characteristics

In the main street, which runs parallel to the sea, there are
still one or two fish restaurants that have preserved something of their original character. Also in this street is the
Ermita de la Virgen de las Nieves (Chapel of the Virgin of the
Snows), which contains the central panel of a 15th c. Flemish triptych of the Virgin and Child; the two side panels are
in the parish church in Agaete. Once a year, during the
Bajada de la Rama (4–7 August), the three parts are brought
together.
The village has a small beach of dark-coloured sand.

The village

To the south of the village the Dedo de Dios (Finger of God),
a curiously shaped pinnacle of rock, rises out of the sea just
off the coast.

* Dedo de Dios

Puerto de Mogán   D2

Altitude: sea level

Puerto de Mogán, the western outpost of the tourist area on
the south coast of Gran Canaria, lies at the mouth of the
Barranco de Mogán, one of the most fertile valleys on the
island.
In recent years Puerto de Mogán has developed with light-
ning speed. At the beginning of the eighties it was occupied
only by a few fishermen and their families, but since then
a considerable holiday development (*urbanización*) has
come into being.

Situation and
characteristics

Two worlds now meet in Puerto de Mogán; on the one hand
the modest houses and shacks of the local fishermen, on
the other the trim white and green houses of the holiday
resort with its marina. The new development, situated
directly on the sea and sometimes called Little Venice,
shows that Gran Canaria is not solely interested in mass
tourism but can cater for more individual and discrimi-
nating tastes. Unfortunately Puerto de Mogán lacks a good
sandy beach; the little bay is stony.
At the north end of the village is a tree nursery where
specimen trees can be bought.

The village

117

Puerto de Mogán

The old Puerto de Mogán . . .

. . . and the new

Marina, Puerto Rico

Puerto Rico   D2

Altitude: sea level

Puerto Rico, on the south-west coast of Gran Canaria, is, like Playa del Inglés and San Agustín (see entries), a purely holiday town; but it is considerably quieter than the tourist resorts farther east. It attracts visitors who are less interested in night life than in an extensive range of sports facilities.

Situation and characteristics

Puerto Rico lies in a sheltered bay surrounded by rock walls rising to a height of 100 m (330 ft). The apartment blocks reach up almost to the top of the hills, and with the new hotels now under construction the resort will have more than 30,000 beds for visitors. In spite of this Puerto Rico has an air of greater openness and elegance than Playa del Inglés. Not surprisingly, therefore, the moorings in its marina were very quickly taken up.

The resort

One disadvantage is that the small sandy beach is usually crowded, and even in the water swimmers, wind-surfers and pleasure craft have to take care to avoid collisions.

*Roque Nublo   C3

The Roque Nublo (Cloud Rock; 1803 m/5916 ft) lies in the centre of Gran Canaria, a few miles west of the Pozo de las

Situation and topography

Nieves (see entry). Its bizarre shape makes it a prominent landmark. This 80 m (260 ft) high pinnacle rising out of a flat-topped hill is a column of harder rock left after the erosion of the surrounding softer rock. To the ancient Canarians it was a sacred spot.

The Roque Nublo in its wild and romantic setting can be reached only on foot, with some stiff climbing. Good starting-points are Ayacata and La Culata.

San Agustín   D3

Altitude: sea level

Situation and characteristics

The hotel town of San Agustín, in the south of Gran Canaria, is gradually coalescing with the resort of Playa del Inglés (see entry), 2 km (1¼ miles) west. It has the only gaming casino on the island (though the possibility of licensing others is under consideration).

The town

There is no old quarter in San Agustín: it is a town of hotels and tourist facilities, though a rather quieter place than its neighbour Playa del Inglés. It has a number of small sandy bays.

Sioux City

A few miles north-west of San Agustín, in the Barranco del Aguila, is Sioux City, a reconstruction of a town in the old American West. With its saloons, its church, its bank, its prison and many other buildings it has been the setting of a number of television films. It is normally open to the public, with Wild West shows (demonstrations of lassoing, shooting, knife-throwing, etc.) twice daily (at 12 noon and 6 p.m.).

San Bartolomé de Tirajana   C3

Altitude: 887 m (2910 ft)
Population (district): 53,000

Situation and characteristics

The village of San Bartolomé de Tirajana lies on the edge of the Caldera de Tirajana, on the south side of Gran Canaria's central massif. It is the chief place in the largest local government district (*municipio*; area 334.5 sq. km/129 sq. miles) on the island. Since the tourist resorts of Maspalomas, Playa del Inglés and San Agustín all lie within the district, it has developed enormously and the population has soared (in 1950 it was barely 9000).

The inhabitants' main source of income is fruit-growing (almonds, plums, apricots, cherries). The fruit is mainly used in the production of fruit brandies and liqueurs.

The village

San Bartolomé is still a relatively unspoiled farming village. The abundance of greenery in and around the village

The mountain world of San Bartolomé de Tirajana

contrasts sharply with the otherwise barren mountain landscape.

San Nicolás de Tolentino   C2

Altitude: 64 m (210 ft)
Population (district): 7500

To get to San Nicolás de Tolentino, situated in the west of
Gran Canaria 5 km (3 miles) from the sea, still involves a
fairly lengthy journey. In the past its contact with the outside world was almost exclusively through the little port of
Puerto de la Aldea.
Although the village lies in a fertile valley – in which, in
addition to tomatoes, potatoes and bananas, pawpaws,
avocados and mangoes are also grown – the shortage
of water limits the possibility of agricultural development.
Little use can be made of the ground-water, which is
drawn from wells, for it is too brackish for most crops, and
the large reservoirs in the surrounding area are frequently
dry.

Situation and
characteristics

San Nicolás de Tolentino is a long straggling village of
whitewashed houses. In between the houses are windmills
which pump up the ground-water.

The village

121

Santa Brígida

B3/4

Altitude: 509 m (1670 ft)
Population (district): 11,500

Situation and
characteristics

Santa Brígida, 15 km (9 miles) south-west of Las Palmas, is a
kind of outlying villa suburb of the capital. Its altitude – it is
always rather cooler here than in Las Palmas – make it a
favoured place of residence for wealthy businessmen.
The Santa Brígida area produces one of the best red wines
on the island.

The town

The houses of Santa Brígida are scattered over the slopes of
the hills and some of the villas are set in large gardens. Tall
eucalyptus trees add variety to the landscape.

La Atalaya

The village of La Atalaya, 5 km (3 miles) west of Santa
Brígida, is famed for its pottery, which is still produced in
the traditional way without the use of a wheel. Since the
village is included in almost every organised tour of the
island, however, the ware is now mass-produced.
On the outskirts of the village are a number of relatively
comfortable cave dwellings, some of which have ordinary
house-fronts built on to them.

Santa Lucía: the church . . .

. . . and old cannon in the museum

Santa Lucía   C3

Altitude: 701 m (2300 ft)
Population (district): 26,500

The picturesque village of Santa Lucía lies on the edge of
the Caldera de Tirajana, a few miles east of San Bartolomé
de Tirajana (see entry). It is a popular stop on island coach
tours.

Situation and
characteristics

Santa Lucía's domed church, rather mosque-like in appear-
ance, is a prominent feature of the landscape. Around the
church are the whitewashed houses of the village and large
numbers of palms.
The main attraction is the private museum in the Hao Restaurant, which has a collection of fossils and relics of the
ancient Canarians; one of the rooms is furnished in 17th c.
Canarian, style. In the garden are a number of old cannon.

The village

Fortaleza Grande

3 km (2 miles) south of Santa Lucía, on the west side of
C 815, is the Fortaleza Grande, a rock formation in the shape
of a castle. To the ancient Canarians this was a sacred spot,
and in April 1483, during the Spanish conquest, they
entrenched themselves here until persuaded to surrender
by their former *guanarteme* (king), Tenesor Semidan (see
Gáldar). The event is still commemorated every year on 29
April with open-air religious services and other ceremonies.

Santa María de Guía   B3

Altitude: 186 m (610 ft)
Population (district): 12,000

Santa María de Guía (Guía for short) lies in the north-west of
Gran Canaria, 2 km (1¼ miles) east of Gáldar (see entry).
The two little towns have a long tradition of rivalry. Guía
was founded at the end of the 15th c. as a kind of "suburb"
of Gáldar to house incoming settlers from Spain; in 1526 it
became an independent town. Guía can claim one advantage over Gáldar; it was the birthplace of the Canarian
sculptor Luján Pérez, whose statues of saints are to be
found in all the major churches in the Canaries.
Guía is famed for its *queso de flor* ("flower cheese"), so
called because juice from the flowers of artichokes is added
to the goat's milk from which the cheese is made. This gives
the cheese an aromatic taste and prevents it from becoming
hard after long keeping.

Situation and
characteristics

Santa María de Guía is a lively little town of narrow streets,
now almost joined to Gáldar.
The parish church shows neo-classical influence. Some of
the many statues it contains are by Luján Pérez; the most
important is a figure of Nuestra Señora de las Mercedes.

The town

Sardina

See Gáldar

Tafira   B4

Altitude: 300–400 m (1000–1300 ft)
Population: 3000

Situation and
characteristics

Tafira, 8 km (5 miles) south-west of Las Palmas, is, like Santa Brígida (see entry), a kind of villa suburb of the capital. The town is in two parts, Tafira Baja and Tafira Alta (Lower and Upper Tafira).
The main reason for visiting Tafira is to see the Jardín Canario.

The town

The little town straggles for some 3 km (2 miles) along the four-lane highway which runs up from Las Palmas to Vega de San Mateo. Many of the houses show evident signs of wealth.

**Jardín Canario (Jardín Botánico Canario Viera y Clavijo)

Open daily 9 a.m.–6 p.m.;
admission free

The Jardín Canario (Canarian Garden) is in the hamlet of La Calzada, below Tafira Alta. The main entrance to this

Succulents in the Jardín Canario

beautiful botanic garden is on the road from Las Palmas to Santa Brígida (C 811); there is another entrance on the Tamaraceite–Santa Brígida road. The garden was established in 1952 by the Swedish botanist Eric R. Sventenius. Only plants native to the Canaries and the Macaronesian Islands (see p. 12) were planted, and the layout of the garden was designed so far as possible to resemble their natural habitats. The original conception of the garden has been brilliantly realised. Within its extensive grounds groves of palms and dragon trees alternate with areas of grass and beds of flowers. Special attention is paid to the growing of endangered species so as to preserve them from extinction. There is also a large collection of succulents. Associated with the garden are a botanical institute, a nursery and a restaurant.

Telde   B/C4

Altitude: 116 m (381 ft)
Population (district): 64,000

Telde, 15 km (9 miles) south of Las Palmas, is the second largest town on Gran Canaria. There are numbers of industrial establishments in and around the town, but agriculture also makes a contribution to its economy; the principal crops are citrus fruits and sugar-cane.
Telde can look back on a long past. In pre-Hispanic times it was the seat of the *guanarteme* (king) who held sway over the eastern part of the island. After the Spanish conquest the town was notorious for its slave market.

Situation and characteristics

The outskirts of Telde, with their factories, warehouses and large shopping centres, are not particularly inviting. The town centre is an area of bustling activity and streets overcrowded with traffic.
The Barrio San Francisco and the Barrio Los Llanos, in the south of the town, are among the oldest parts of Telde. In San Francisco lived the well-to-do citizens of the town, while Los Llanos was the home of the negro slaves who worked on the surrounding sugar-cane plantations.

The town

The fine church of San Juan Bautista, in the northern part of the town, is built of variegated volcanic stone. The Gothic west front dates from the 16th c.
The church has a beautifully carved Flemish retablo of about 1500 with six scenes from the life of the Virgin. The principal scene (centre, p. 126) depicts the Nativity. Above the retablo is a life-size figure of Christ from Mexico; made from maize pith, it weighs only 5 kg (11 lb). Among the church's other art treasures is a figure of St Bernard by the Italian painter Vicente Carducci (1578–1638).

* Iglesia de San Juan Bautista

The birthplace of Juan de León y Castillo, the engineer responsible for building the harbour of Las Palmas at the end of the 19th c., is now a museum.
(Open Monday to Friday 3–6 p.m.)

Museo León y Castillo

Montaña de las Cuatro Puertas

5 km (3 miles) south of Telde on the road to Ingenio is the Montaña de las Cuatro Puertas ("Hill of the Four Gates"; 319 m/1047 ft). It is possible to drive to within 200 m (220 yd) of the summit, on which are four man-made openings in the rock, leading into an inner chamber which was a cult place of the ancient Canarians. The open space in front of the cave was a *tagoror* (place of assembly).
On the south side of the hill are other caves, some natural and some hewn out of the rock, which were occupied as dwellings. Traces of steps can be seen on the floor of some of the caves.

Teror   B3

Altitude: 543 m (1782 ft)
Population (district): 9500

The little town of Teror, in the north of Gran Canaria some 20 km (12½ miles) south-west of Las Palmas, is the island's principal religious centre. Its church contains a statue of the Virgen del Pino, patroness of Gran Canaria, whose fiesta on 8 September is a great event in the island's year.
Every Sunday morning there is a busy market in Teror, where the goods offered for sale include not only locally grown fruit and vegetables, peasant bread baked in stone ovens and aromatic cheeses but also clothing and household articles.

Situation and characteristics

Teror is regarded as the island's most typical Canarian town. It has many fascinating old houses with decorated wooden balconies and beautiful patios; some of the housefronts bear coats of arms.
In the centre of the town is the Basílica de Nuestra Señora del Pino. Diagonally opposite it is the Casa de los Patronos de la Virgen del Pino, a well-preserved example of old Canarian architecture dating from about 1600 which now houses a museum. The numerous exhibits in the museum (pictures, weapons, crockery, kitchenware, etc.) and the beautiful patio give a vivid impression of life in the Canaries in earlier days.

** The town

Basílica de Nuestra Señora del Pino

The most important building in Teror is the Basílica de Nuestra Señora del Pino, built on the spot where the Virgin is said to have appeared to Juan Frías, first Bishop of Gran Canaria, on 8 December 1482. Juan Frías saw the Virgin in the branches of a pine tree, which survived until it was blown down by a storm in 1684. The first chapel, built in 1515, was replaced in 1692 by a larger church, which was almost completely destroyed by an explosion in 1718. Only the tower survived, and this was incorporated in the present church, built in 1760–67.

◀ *Retablo in the Iglesia de San Juan Bautista*

The 15th c. statue of the Virgen del Pino, 1 m (just over 3 ft) high, also survived the explosion unscathed. It is now enthroned in an 18th c. silver litter made at La Laguna on Tenerife. The two sides of the Virgin's face are different: one side expresses sorrow, while the other has a gentle smile. Another precious relic is a cross made from the wood of the legendary pine tree, now preserved under glass.

Vega de San Mateo   B3

Altitude: 836 m (2743 ft)
Population (district): 7000

Situation and
characteristics

Vega de San Mateo (often called simply San Mateo) lies in the interior of Gran Canaria 20 km (12½ miles) south-west of Las Palmas. Thanks to the abundance of water in the area the land is intensively cultivated; fruit and vegetables are the principal crops.
The main attraction of San Mateo is its Sunday livestock market, at which goats, pigs, cows and smaller forms of livestock change hands. Cheese, fruit and vegetables are also sold.

The village

In the village square is the Casa-Museo de Cho Zacarías, with a collection of old domestic and agricultural equipment. Attached to the museum are a shop selling a great variety of souvenirs and a restaurant.

Practical Information

Airlines

Iberia,
Avenida Ramírez Béthencourt 8,
Las Palmas; tel. 37 21 11
Gando Airport: tel. 25 41 40
Flights on its subsidiary companies Binter Canarias and
Aviaco can also be booked through Iberia.

On Gran Canaria

British Airways,
Calle Gordillo 13 (1st floor),
Las Palmas; tel. 26 15 86

Iberia,
Veintitrés de Mayo 11,
Puerto del Rosario; tel. 85 05 16

On Fuerteventura

Iberia,
Avenida Rafael González 2,
Arrecife; tel. 81 03 50

On Lanzarote

Air services

Gran Canaria's international airport, the Aeropuerto de
Gando, is situated 20 km (12½ miles) south of Las Palmas.
Airport bus from Iberia terminal, Parque San Telmo,
Avenida Maritima, every 40 minutes from 5.30 a.m.–10 p.m.
Fuerteventura has the Aeropuerto del Rosario, 7 km (4½
miles) south of Puerto del Rosario, and Lanzarote the Aeropuerto de Arrecife, 6 km (4 miles) west of Arrecife. These
airports are used only by international charter flights and
domestic services.

Airports

From the Aeropuerto de Gando on Gran Canaria there
are several flights daily with Iberia or its subsidiaries Aviaco
and Binter Canarias to the islands of Fuerteventura,
Lanzarote, Tenerife and La Palma.
From the Aeropuerto del Rosario on Fuerteventura there
are several flights daily to Gran Canaria, two flights daily to
Tenerife and two or three flights weekly to Lanzarote.
From the Aeropuerto de Arrecife on Lanzarote there are
several flights daily to Gran Canaria and two or three flights
weekly to Fuerteventura.

Inter-island flights

Flying times between the islands range between 25 and
50 minutes. Since fares are relatively low, air travel is a
popular means of transport with the islanders. Seats
should, therefore, be booked in plenty of time, particularly
on public holidays and on flights to the smaller islands.
Excess baggage is sometimes carried free or at a small
extra charge.

Banks

See Currency

Beaches

Gran Canaria, Fuerteventura and Lanzarote – unlike the western Canaries – all have long and beautiful sandy beaches. The beaches on Fuerteventura in particular are a bather's and sunbather's dream. Almost all the best holiday beaches on Gran Canaria are on the south coast; on Lanzarote they are on the south and south-east coasts, on Fuerteventura on the south and north coasts. The best beaches on each island are listed below.

Beaches on Gran Canaria

Arguineguín has only a tiny sandy beach; much more attractive are the swimming pools attached to the hotels.

Arguineguín

North-west of Las Palmas is the Playa de las Canteras, a beautiful beach of light-coloured sand some 2 km (1¼ miles) long. Offshore reefs provide protection from the surf, making bathing entirely safe. Although the beach and the seafront promenade are well kept, the nearness of the city means that the beach can become uncomfortably crowded, particularly at weekends – and the Las Palmas industrial zone begins at the south end of the beach.

Las Palmas

A well-kept beach of white sand extends for 7 km (4½ miles) from the Faro de Maspalomas to San Agustín, flanked by an extraordinary dune landscape which is scheduled as a nature reserve. This fascinating stretch of coast is Gran Canaria's principal tourist attraction, which in winter draws hosts of sun-starved northern Europeans, particularly Germans. Deck chairs, sun umbrellas, pedalos, surfboards, etc., can be hired, and there are plenty of simple snack bars directly on the beach.

Playa del Inglés/Maspalomas

Puerto de las Nieves is the only place in the north-west of Gran Canaria with a reasonably good beach, a stretch of dark-coloured sand 100 m (110 yd) long and 25 m (30 yd) wide which is mostly frequented by local people.

Puerto de las Nieves

Puerto de Mogán has a very modest little sandy beach. If you do not mind a longish walk or a car drive the Playa del Diablillo, south of the village, is to be preferred. This broad beach of white sand attracts individual tourists and is not unduly busy.

Puerto de Mogán

The beach at Puerto Rico – 400 m (440 yd) of artificially built up sand – has one advantage; it is usually sunny

Puerto Rico

◀ *Marina of Puerto Rico*

Beach, Puerto Rico

here even when there are clouds over Maspalomas and Playa del Inglés. Since this happens not infrequently in the winter months, the Puerto Rico beach can get uncomfortably overcrowded then, and even at other times the beach mattresses are packed pretty closely together. Bathers must share the sea with large numbers of wind-surfers, sailing dinghies and yachts. Barrier reefs provide protection from unduly heavy surf.

San Agustín

The beach at San Agustín is modest in comparison with the neighbouring Playa del Inglés. There are a number of small sandy bays, the best of which is the stretch of white sand in front of the Sun Club; elsewhere the sand is dark-coloured.

Beaches on Fuerteventura

Caleta de Fustes, El Castillo

The 500 m (550 yd) long beach of white sand at Caleta de Fustes, sheltered from the strong surf by a promontory, is safe even for children. Many first-time wind-surfers try their skill here. Attractive as this beach is, however, it does not compare with the paradisiac beaches on the north and south coasts of Fuerteventura.

Corralejo

A magnificent sandy beach flanked by extensive dunes extends south from Corralejo for some 10 km (6 miles) almost to the Montaña Roja. Once Corralejo is left behind it is always possible to find a secluded spot. Tourist facilities (hire of beach mattresses, etc.) are to be found only in the

One of Fuerteventura's beautiful lonely beaches

immediate vicinity of the resort. In a strong wind drifting sand may be a nuisance.

The sandy beaches north and south of the fishing village of Cotillo, on the north-west coast of Fuerteventura, are almost untouched by the hand of man. The strong winds which blow here make this a favourite area with wind-surfers.

Cotillo

Here you will find sand and sea as far as the eye can reach. From Morro del Jable a magnificent sandy beach extends for almost 20 km (12½ miles) to the Punta de los Molinillos, with innumerable lonely and secluded bays. Only in the vicinity of the town or the occasional holiday villages are there any large numbers of people. Some visitors build stone shelters to protect them from drifting sand, complete with boards declaring their ownership.

Jandía/Morro del Jable

The 600 m (660 yd) long beach at the Parador Nacional is frequented mainly by local people.

Playa Blanca

The Playa de Cofete and Playa de Barlovento on the south-west coast of Fuerteventura are still largely untouched by tourism. They can be reached only in a cross-country vehicle. There is sometimes a very strong surf here.

Playa de Cofete/
Playa de Barlovento

Beaches on Lanzarote

Although some of the most attractive hotel complexes in the Canaries are to be found on the Costa Teguise, a few

Costa Teguise

133

miles north of Arrecife, there are only tiny stretches of sand for the visitors who come here. The Playa Bastián is 200 m (220 yd) long, the beach at the luxury hotel Las Salinas 300 m (330 yd) long.

La Caleta

The Playa de San Juan to the west of La Caleta is relatively small, but the Playa de Famara to the east is one of the longest sandy beaches on the island. Disadvantages are the wind, which often brings drift sand, and the strong surf.

Playa Blanca

The beach at Playa Blanca itself is tiny, but bathers are better catered for on the beaches which lie between 2 and 5 km (1¼ and 3 miles) to the east of the resort. Here there is a succession of sandy bays, the finest of which is the Playa de Papagayo. Though these beaches now attract many more holidaymakers than in the past it is still possible to find a secluded place in the sun.

Puerto del Carmen

The longest stretch of beach on the island extends east from Puerto del Carmen for 8 km (5 miles). The character of the beach varies from place to place; the best sandy beach – which tends on that account to be overcrowded – is the Playa Blanca. The Playa de Pocillos is frequented by local people at weekends. Unfortunately the main road runs close to the beach at many points.

Beaches on Graciosa

Many visitors take a day trip from Lanzarote to the little island of Graciosa for the sake of its beautiful lonely sandy beaches. The best of them extend to the west of Caleta del Sebo, where for mile after mile there is nothing but the beach and the dunes.

Beaches on Lobos

Visitors who want to spend only a day on the beach will not find it worth while to cross from Fuerteventura to Lobos. The Playa de la Arena and Playa del Sobrado cannot compare with Fuerteventura's own beautiful beaches.

Naturist beaches

Topless sunbathing is perfectly normal in the tourist resorts on the islands, although it may attract attention on beaches mainly frequented by local people. Nude bathing is usually tolerated on the remoter beaches.
On Gran Canaria naturists should make for the dunes at Maspalomas and Playa del Inglés, on Lanzarote for the beaches to the east of Playa Blanca. On Fuerteventura with its many lonely beaches nude bathing is possible almost anywhere outside the resorts.

Playa de las Canteras, Las Palmas

Boat services

See Transport

Books

Newspaper kiosks and supermarkets on Gran Canaria, Fuerteventura and Lanzarote offer a limited range of light fiction in English. A wider selection can be found in the larger bookshops and department stores in Las Palmas. Transport costs mean that books tends to be dearer than at home.

Bus services

See Transport

Camping

Camping Guantánamo,
La Playa de Tauro,
Puerto Rico (Gran Canaria);
tel. 24 17 01

Camping sites

Practical Information

Camping Temisas,
Lomo de la Cruz
(on the road from Agüimes to San Bartolomé de Tirajana on Gran Canaria);
tel. 79 81 49.

On Fuerteventura and Lanzarote there are no official camping sites.

"Camping sauvage"

As a rule the authorities turn a blind eye to "wild" camping. Occasional tents can be seen along the coasts of Gran Canaria, Fuerteventura and Lanzarote.

Caravans

In Spain it is normally permitted to spend one night on the same spot in a trailer or motor caravan.

Car rental

Gran Canaria

Avis,
Calle Juan Manuel Durán 13, Las Palmas;
tel. 26 55 72
and
Edificio Bayuca, Av. Alféreces Provisionales, Playa del Inglés;
tel. 76 54 26
(Also at the airport)

Hertz,
Calle de Sagasta 29, Las Palmas;
tel. 26 39 33
(Also at the airport)

Europcar/InterRent,
Los Martinez de Escobar 24, Las Palmas;
tel. 26 57 57
and
Edificio Bayuca, Av. Alféreces Provisionales, Playa del Inglés;
tel. 76 55 00
(Also at the airport and in Puerto Rico)

Fuerteventura

Avis,
Calle 1 de Mayo 5, Puerto del Rosario;
tel. 85 02 61
(Also in Corralejo)

Hertz,
Aeropuerto, Puerta del Rosario;
tel. 86 62 59
(Also in Morro Jable, Corralejo and in the Centro Commercial Tennis, Playa Paratso)

Lanzarote

Avis,
Aeropuerto, Arrecife;
tel. 81 22 56

Europcar/InterRent,
in the San Antonio Hotel, Puerto del Carmen;
tel. 82 50 50
(Also at the airport)

For a car in the lowest category the international car rental firms charge between 3000 and 4000 pesetas a day according to the period of hire. The rates usually cover unlimited mileage.
Comprehensive insurance costs about 600 pesetas a day. These rates are often undercut by the numerous smaller rental firms.

Rates

Chemists

Chemists' shops are open Monday to Friday 9 a.m.–1 p.m. and 4–8 p.m., Saturday 9 a.m.–1 p.m. At other times there is always a "duty pharmacy" open in places of any size on Gran Canaria. The address of the duty pharmacy is given in a notice headed "Farmacia de Guardia" in every chemist's window. After 10 p.m. only medicines on prescription are issued.

Church services

Holy Trinity Church (Anglican) is at the corner of Calle Brasil and Calle Rafael Ramírez.
The Templo Ecuménico (Oecumenical Church) in Playa del Inglés (near the Kasbah shopping centre) is used in turn by different religious denominations. The times of Catholic or Protestant services in English are given on a notice at the church door.

Consulates

Edificio Cataluña,
Calle de Luis Morote 6 (3rd floor),
Las Palmas;
tel. 26 25 08

United Kingdom

Calle José Franchy Roca 5,
Las Palmas;
tel. 27 12 59

United States

Currency

The unit of currency is the Spanish peseta (pta). There are banknotes for 500 (being withdrawn), 1000, 2000, 5000 and 10,000 pesetas and coins in denominations of 1, 5, 10, 25, 50, 100, 200 and 500 pesetas.

Exchange rates (subject to fluctuation) can be found in the Press, at banks, tourist offices and hotel reception desks.

Exchange rates

Visitors to Spain may take in an unlimited sum in pesetas, and may take out a maximum of 100,000 pesetas.

Currency regulations

There are no restrictions on the import of foreign currency, but to avoid any difficulties on leaving the country it is advisable to declare any large sums taken in. Foreign currency may be exported up to the equivalent of 500,000 pesetas, or a larger amount if declared on entry.

Eurocheques

Eurocheques can be drawn for amounts not exceeding 25,000 pesetas.
If you lose your Eurocheques and/or Eurocard you should inform your bank by telephone and confirm in writing within 7 days. The local police should also be informed.

Girobank

Account-holders of the British National Girobank, with Postcheques and a special card, can draw the equivalent of £65 at a time from Spanish post offices.

Credit cards

Banks, the larger hotels and better-class restaurants, car rental firms and many shops accept the major charge and credit cards (American Express, Diners Club, Access, Eurocard, Visa, etc.).

Changing money

Money can be changed at banks (open Monday to Friday 9 a.m.–2 p.m., Saturday 9 a.m.–1 p.m.), exchange offices, travel agents and the reception desk in the larger hotels. It is always changed at the official rate, but commission charges may vary considerably.

Customs regulations

Personal effects and other everyday requirements may be taken into Spain without payment of duty. In addition there are duty-free allowances, for persons over 15, of 1000 grams of coffee or 400 grams of instant coffee and 200 grams of tea or 80 grams of tea extract, and, for persons over 17, of 1½ litres of alcoholic drinks over 22% vol. (38.8 ° proof) or 3 litres of alcoholic drinks not over 22% or 3 litres of sparkling wine and 5 litres of wine, together with 300 cigarettes or 75 cigars or 400 grams of tobacco. Persons over 15 may also take in gifts and other articles to the value of 48,000 pesetas.

Doctors

See Medical care

Drinks

See Food and drink

Electricity

Normally 220 volts. In the large hotels the power sockets take plugs of normal European type (with prongs which are thinner and set slightly farther apart than in the British type). Appliances with plugs of non-European type will require adaptors. Outside the large hotels there may often be sockets of a different type, for which adaptors can be bought locally.

Emergency calls

Gran Canaria: tel. 20 71 22 Lanzarote: tel. 81 48 58	Fire service (Bomberos)
On all islands: tel. 091	Police (Policia)
Gran Canaria: Las Palmas, tel. 092; San Agustín, tel. 76 24 12 Fuerteventura: tel. 85 06 35 Lanzarote: tel. 81 13 17	Municipal police (Policia municipal)
Emergencies, on all islands: tel. 23 00 00 Ambulance transport, on all islands: tel. 24 59 21	Red Cross (Cruz Roja)
Gran Canaria: Las Palmas, tel. 24 51 57; San Agustín, tel. 76 10 22 Fuerteventura: tel. 85 13 76 Lanzarote: tel. 81 20 62	Casualty stations (Casas de socorro)
See Medical care	Hospitals

Events

In this section we list only the most important events and those most likely to be of interest to visitors.

Patronal festivals (the feasts of the local patron saints) usually involve not only a pilgrimage but a variety of secular activities – Canarian wrestling (*lucha canaria*), a fair, musical performances, boat trips, etc.

Las Palmas/Gran Canaria: Cabalgada de los Reyes Magos (Cavalcade of the Three Kings).	5 January
Las Palmas/Gran Canaria: Festival of Classical Music, with internationally known artistes; events in Teatro Pérez Galdós.	January/February
Many places: Carnival. The most lavish celebrations are in Las Palmas and Playa del Inglés/Maspalomas.	February
Tejeda and Valsequillo/Gran Canaria: Almond Blossom Festival.	

Practical Information

March/April	Many places: Semana Santa (Holy Week), with numerous processions and other religious and secular celebrations.
29 April	Las Palmas/Gran Canaria: Anniversary of the union of Gran Canaria with the kingdom of Castile.
April/May	Las Palmas/Gran Canaria: Spanish Festival (theatre and ballet).
June	Many places: Corpus Christi, with processions passing over magnificent carpets of flowers (particularly splendid in Las Palmas and Arucas on Gran Canaria).
24 June	Las Palmas/Gran Canaria: Anniversary of the foundation of the town (numerous ceremonies and celebrations).
	Haría/Lanzarote: Fiesta de San Juan (patronal festival).
2 July	Pájara/Fuerteventura: Fiesta de la Virgen de Regla (patronal festival).
14 July	Betancuria/Fuerteventura: Fiesta de la Buenaventura (patronal festival).
16 July	Las Palmas, Gáldar, San Nicolás de Tolentino/Gran Canaria; Corralejo, Morro del Jable/Fuerteventura; Yaiza, Teguise/Lanzarote: Fiesta de Nuestra Señora del Carmen (patronal festival).
25 July	Gáldar and San Bartolomé/Gran Canaria: Fiesta de Santiago (St James: patronal festival).
4 August	Agaete/Gran Canaria: Bajada de la Rama (procession).
15 August	Santa María de Guía/Gran Canaria: Fiesta de Santa María (patronal festival).
24 August	San Bartolomé/Lanzarote: Fiesta de San Bartolomé (patronal festival).
25 August	Arrecife/Lanzarote: Fiesta de San Ginés (patronal festival): the high point of the year, with religious and secular celebrations.
6–8 September	Teror/Gran Canaria: Fiesta de la Virgen del Pino (a typical pilgrimage).
15 September	Tinajo/Lanzarote: Fiesta de la Virgen de los Volcanes.
3rd Saturday in September	Many places on Fuerteventura: Fiesta de la Virgen de la Peña, the feast of the island's patroness, with a pilgrimage to Vega del Río de Palma (Betancuria).
6 October	Las Palmas/Gran Canaria: Fiesta in the harbour district, commemorating the victory over Sir Francis Drake's fleet in 1595.
7 October	Puerto del Rosario/Fuerteventura: Fiesta de la Virgen del Rosario (patronal festival), celebrated in the harbour.

Las Palmas/Gran Canaria: Fiesta de Nuestra Señora de la Luz (pilgrimage and boat procession in sea).	2nd Saturday in October
Tuineje/Fuerteventura: Fiesta de San Miguel (patronal festival).	13 October
Many places, particularly Las Palmas/Gran Canaria: Fiestas de Navidad (a varied programme of pre-Christmas and Christmas celebrations, with exhibitions and other events).	December

Excursions

Holidaymakers in the main tourist centres on Gran Canaria are offered a wide range of coach tours by local agencies. Among the most popular excursions are a tour of the island, shorter trips into the central range of hills, to Agaete, Tejeda and the Palmitos Park, and shopping trips to Las Palmas or, on Sundays, to markets in some of the smaller places on the island.
On Lanzarote and Fuerteventura there are tours of the island.

By coach

There is no difficulty about touring any of the islands with a hired car (see Car rental, Suggested itineraries).
Another way of getting to know the islands is to go on one of the jeep safaris into remote and unspoiled areas which cannot be reached in an ordinary car.

By car

A wide variety of boat trips is on offer, ranging from short trips along the coast and day trips to cruises lasting several days.

By boat

On Gran Canaria there are trips to watch the shark-fishing and sailing trips on the "Pegasus" (from Puerto Rico), or you can have a day trip from Las Palmas to Santa Cruz de Tenerife on the jetfoil, which takes only 80 minutes for the crossing. In view of the greater distances involved, day trips from Gran Canaria to other islands are not worth while.
If you are staying on either Fuerteventura or Lanzarote, which are close together, you should not miss the chance of a trip to the other island. The travel operators offer combined boat and coach trips, but it is perfectly easy to organise your own trip: there are several ferries a day between Corralejo on Fuerteventura and Playa Blanca on Lanzarote, and a car can be hired on the other side. There is no particular attraction in a whole day in either Corralejo or Playa Blanca.
For a quiet day's bathing you can take a boat trip from Fuerteventura (Corralejo) to the little island of Lobos or from Morro del Jable to the Punta de Jandía.
On Lanzarote there is also the possibility of a boat trip to the island of Graciosa.

Since each of the Canary Islands has its own distinctive character and air fares are relatively low (see Air services), a day trip by air to one of the other islands offers variety of scenery and interest at very reasonable cost. Combined air

By air

and coach tours can be booked through travel agencies. For a sightseeing flight over Gran Canaria, apply to the Aeroclub in San Agustín (tel. 76 24 47).

Also on offer are short trips by air to the Gambia and to Marrakesh in Morocco.

Food and drink

Meals and meal-times

In the Canaries, as in the rest of Spain, a light breakfast (*desayuno*) is followed by a substantial lunch (*almuerzo*) and dinner (*cena*). The two main meals are usually of three courses.

The Canarians usually have lunch between 1 and 3.30 p.m., dinner between 8 and 10.30 p.m. The large hotels and restaurants, however, now often serve meals at the rather earlier times to which most visitors are accustomed.

Canarian cuisine

Elaborately prepared dishes are not to be looked for in the cuisine of the Canaries, but visitors will be surprised to discover how good the local seafood or the substantial meat dishes can be. As in mainland Spain, much use is made of olive oil, garlic and a variety of herbs.

Restaurants and hotels tend to offer an international cuisine, usually of no more than standard quality. In the smaller places and in country restaurants it is well worth while trying some of the local dishes.

Tapas

For a snack between meals or as a preliminary to a meal there are the inevitable *tapas* (appetisers). Bars and bodegas as well as restaurants offer a selection of these tasty titbits, which may include goat's-milk cheese (*queso blanco*), olives, smoked ham (*jamón*), small pieces of fried fish and other types of seafood.

Gofio

Gofio, made from roasted wheat, maize or barley flour, was the staple food of the ancient Canarians and is still an essential element in the diet of the islanders, though it is unlikely to appear on a restaurant menu. It is eaten with various dishes in place of bread, and can be either sweet or salt.

Soups

Visitors staying in coastal resorts should try the local fish soup (*sopa de pescado*), which at its best will include a variety of different kinds of fish, mussels and other shellfish, together with vegetables. *Escaldón* is a thick soup made with gofio, *potaje de verduras* a substantial vegetable soup.

Fish dishes

Fish (*pescado*) features prominently in the cuisine of the Canaries, usually grilled or fried. *Vieja* is a very tasty fish similar to carp; it may be either fresh or dried. Also popular is *sancocho* (dried fish parboiled with potatoes, onions and garlic). Other fish dishes found almost everywhere are *calamares a la romana* (deep-fried cuttlefish rings) and *gambas a la plancha* (grilled prawns).

Meat dishes

Visitors who prefer meat (*carne*) will find a choice of pork (*cerdo*), mutton (*carnero*), lamb (*cordero*) and rabbit (*conejo*), which may be either grilled or roasted. There are also typical Canarian meat dishes with unusual combinations of ingredients, among them *puchero*, a stew of different kinds of meat and vegetables, varying according to season; for a special occasion puchero is made with seven different kinds of meat.

Canarian fish and meat dishes are given their particular flavour by the piquant sauce called *mojo*, made from local herbs, garlic, vinegar and oil. *Mojo rojo* (red mojo) also includes saffron and red peppers, *mojo verde* (green mojo) parsley and coriander.

Mojo

An essential feature of the Canarian menu is *papas arruga-das* – jacket potatoes boiled in well salted water. They are eaten in their jackets, which have a white deposit of salt.

Papas arrugadas

The people of the Canaries like sweet things, and desserts are always included in the meal. Very tempting, but with a high calorie content, are *bienmesabe* (whipped almond cream with egg and honey), *turrones* (almond cakes), *flan* (crême caramel), *frangollo* (a sweet made of maize flour and milk), and of course ices (*helados*) and fresh fruit. An attractive speciality in some restaurants is flambé bananas.

Desserts

The local mineral water (*agua mineral*) is excellent; it may be either still (*sin gas*) or carbonated (*con gas*). Firgas (Gran Canaria) is famed for its mineral water, which is sold in all the eastern Canaries.
Beer (*cerveza*) and of course wine (*vino*) are commonly drunk with meals. The local country wine (*vino del país*), either red or white, is rarely to be had: it is normally blended with wine from mainland Spain. The Canaries are cele-brated for their Malvasía (Malmsey) and muscatel wines.

Drinks

The meal will usually end with coffee, either *café solo* (with-out milk), *café cortado* (with a little milk) or *café con leche* (white coffee). A further variant is *carajillo* (black coffee with a shot of brandy or rum).

Getting to the eastern Canaries

There are several flights daily by Iberia, the Spanish national airline, from London to Las Palmas (Gran Canaria) and four flights weekly from London to Arrecife (Lanzarote). It is also possible to fly from international airports round the world to Madrid and get a domestic flight from there.

By air

Iberia and its subsidiaries Aviaco and Binter Canarias have several flights daily between Gran Canaria, Fuerteventura and Lanzarote.

There are also numerous charter flights to the eastern Ca-naries from London and other European cities, usually as part of a package which includes accommodation but leaves visitors free to spend their time as they wish.

There is a weekly car ferry service run by the Spanish shipping line Compañía Trasmediterránea from Cádiz via

By sea

143

Santa Crus de Tenerife to Las Palmas (Gran Canaria) and Arrecife (Lanzarote). Further information can be obtained from the agents of the Compañía Trasmediterránea.

Compañía
Trasmediterránea

Agents in the United Kingdom:

Melia Travel,
12 Dover Street,
London W1X 4NS;
tel. (01) 499 6731

Hospitals

See Medical care

Hotels

Hoteles, hostales,
pensiones

Spanish hotels are officially classified according to function and quality into various types: *hoteles* (singular *hotel*; accommodation with or without meals, own restaurant); *hoteles-apartamentos* (like *hoteles*, but with flats or chalets); *hostales* (singular *hostal*; more modest establishments, with or without meals); and *pensiones* (singular *pensión*; guest-houses, fewer rooms, full board only). Hotels, apartment hotels and *hostales* may be described as *residencias* (no restaurant, but usually providing breakfast).

Paradores

These State-run hotels (*paradores nacionales de turismo*), situated at places of particular tourist interest, are usually beautifully sited, offer every comfort and amenity and have well-trained staff.

Categories

Hotels and other types of accommodation are classed in five categories, ranging from luxury hotels (five stars) to the most modest hotels, hostales or pensiones (one star).

The following list of hotels is based on this system of classification. It gives the address, telephone number and number of rooms; establishments with swimming pools are indicated by the letters SP. The list consists mainly of hotels; hostales are included only where there is insufficient hotel accommodation.

Tariffs

Hotel tariffs vary considerably according to season. The rates given in the following table (in pesetas) are a guide to the cost of an overnight stay for two persons (with breakfast): the rate for a single room ranges between 60 and 80 per cent of the tariff for a double room.

Category Double room
***** 13,000–35,000 ptas
**** 9000–25,000 ptas
*** 5000–15,000 ptas
** 2000–7000 ptas
* 1500–5000 ptas

Hotel Santa Catalina, Las Palmas

Hotels on Gran Canaria

**Princesa Guayarmina, Calle los Berrazales, tel. 89 80 09, 27 rooms, SP   Agaete

*****Steinberger Hotel La Canaria, tel. 73 60 60, 246 r., SP   Arguineguin

**Bella Arehucas, Calle Panchito Hernández 10, tel. 60 06 51, 10 r.   Arucas

*****Meliá Cristina, Calle Gomera 6, tel. 26 76 00, 316 r., SP   Las Palmas
*****Reina Isabel, Calle Alfredo L. Jones 40, tel. 26 01 00, 234 r., SP
*****Santa Catalina, Parque Doramas, tel. 24 30 40, 208 r., SP
****Concorde, Calle Tomás Miller 85, tel. 26 27 50, 127 r., SP
****Iberia Sol, Av. Marítima del Norte, tel. 36 11 33, 298 r., SP
****Imperial Playa, Calle Ferreras 1, tel. 26 48 54, 173 r.
****Los Bardinos, Calle Eduardo Benot 3, tel. 26 61 00, 215 r., SP
****Rocamar, Calle Lanzarote 10, tel. 26 56 00, 87 r.
****Sansofe, Calle Portugal 68, tel. 26 4758, 101 r.
****Tigaday, Calle Ripoche 4, tel. 26 47 20, 160 r., SP
***Astoria Club, Calle Pelayo 17, tel. 26 90 82, 160 r., SP
***Atlanta, Calle Alfredo L. Jones 37, tel. 26 50 62, 58 r.
***Fataga, Calle Néstor de la Torre 21, tel. 24 04 08, 92 r.
***Gran Canaria, Paseo de las Canteras 38, tel. 27 50 78, 90 r.

***Miraflor, Calle Doctor Grau Bassas 21, tel. 26 16 00, 78 r.
***Náutilus, Paseo de las Canteras 5, tel. 26 32 74, 49 r.
***Olympia, Calle Doctor Grau Bassas 1, tel. 26 17 20, 41 r.
***Parque, Muelle de las Palmas 2, tel. 36 80 00, 119 r.
***Rosalia, Calle Doctor Miguel Rosas 3, tel. 26 58 50, 45 r.
***Sorimba, Calle Portugal 24, tel. 22 15 18 45 r.
***Utiaca, Calle Albareda 35, tel. 27 01 00, 79 r.
**Atlántida, Calle Nicolás Estévanez 64, tel. 27 63 56, 36 r.
**Cactus, Calle Juan Rejón 73, tel. 26 29 00, 32 r.
**Funchal, Calle de los Martínez de Escobar 66, tel. 26 55 78, 35 r.
**Germán, Calle Faro 66, tel. 26 58 74, 11 r.
**Majórica, Calle Ripoche 22, tel. 26 28 78, 38 r.
**Pujol, Calle Salvador Cuyás 5, tel. 27 44 33, 48 r.
**Valencia, Calle Valencia 64, tel. 24 84 47, 39 r.
*Los Angeles, Calle Montevideo 3, tel. 26 18 16, 20 r.
*Madrid, Plaza Cairasco 2, tel. 36 06 64, 39 r.

Playa del Inglés/
Maspalomas

*****Maspalomas Oasis, Playa de Maspalomas, tel. 76 01 70, 342 r., SP
****Apolo, Avenida de E.E.U.U. 28, tel. 76 00 58, 115 r., SP
****Catarina Playa, Avenida de Tirajana 1, tel. 76 28 12, 402 r., SP
****Corona Caserio, Avenida de Italia 8, tel. 76 10 50, 106 r., SP
****Don Gregory, Calle de las Tabaibas 11, tel. 76 26 62, 241 r., SP
****Ifa Hotel Dunamar, Calle Helsinki 8, tel. 76 12 00, 184 r., SP
****Ifa Hotel Faro de Maspalomas, Playa de Maspalomas, tel. 76 04 62, 188 r., SP
****Las Margaritas, Avenida de Gran Canaria 38, tel. 76 11 22, 323 r., SP
****Lucana, Plaza del Sol, tel. 76 27 00, 167 r., SP
****Maspalomas Palm Beach, Avenida del Oasis, tel. 76 29 20, 358 r.
****Río Palmera, Avenida de E.E.U.U. 1, tel. 76 64 00, 231 r., SP
***Buenaventura Playa, Plaza Ansite, tel. 76 16 50, 716 r.
***Continental, Avenida de Italia 2, tel. 76 00 33, 383 r., SP
***Eugenia Victoria, Avenida de Gran Canaria 26, tel. 76 25 00, 400 r., SP
***Parque Tropical, Avenida de Italia 1, tel. 76 07 12, 235 r., SP
***Playa del Inglés, Avenida de Italia 27, tel. 76 08 00, 189 r.
***Rey Carlos, Avenida de Tirajana 14, tel. 76 01 16, 160 r.
***Waikiki, Avenida de Gran Canaria, tel. 76 23 00, 508 r., SP
**Escorial, Avenida de Italia 6, tel. 76 13 68, 251 r.
** Inter Club Atlantic, Calle Jazmines 2, tel. 76 09 50, 105 r., SP.

Mogán

****Revoli, Avenida de Mogán, 74 50 01, 181 r., SP
**Puerto Plata, Avenida de la Cornisa, tel. 74 51 50, 246 r., SP
*La Riviera, Playa del Cura, tel. 74 51 31, 150 r.

Puerto Rico

***Río Piedras, Avenida del Ancia 2, tel. 74 58 98, 98 apts, SP
**Martinica, Avenida del Valle 6, tel. 74 50 41, 28 apts, SP
**Tindaya, Calle Tasártico 17, tel. 74 57 25, 86 apts, SP

San Agustín

*****Meliá Tamarindos, Calle las Retama 3, tel. 76 26 00, 318 r., SP
****Bahía Feliz, Playa de Tarajalillo, tel. 76 46 00, 255 r.

Hotel Bahía Feliz, San Agustín

****Costa Canaria, Calle las Retamas, tel. 76 02 00, 158 r.,
SP
****Folias, Calle las Retamas 17, tel. 76 24 50, 79 r.
***Beverly Park, Calle Hamburgo, tel. 76 17 50, 497 r., SP
***Ifa Beach, Calle Jazmines 25, tel. 76 51 00, 200 r.
**Inter Club Atlántic, Calle Jazmines 2, tel. 76 09 50, 105 r.,
SP

La Posada, Caldera de Bandama, tel. 35 12 90, 25 r.   Santa Brígida

*Los Frailes, Carretera del Centro (km 8), tel. 35 12 06, 26 r.   Tafira Alta

Hotels on Fuerteventura

****Tres Islas, Playa de Corralejo, tel. 86 60 00, 356 r., SP   Corralejo
***Oliva Playa, Playa de Corralejo, tel. 86 61 00, 386 r., SP
*Corralejo, Playa de Corralejo, tel. 86 62 28, 19 r.

***Los Gorriones, tel. 87 08 50, 309 r., SP   Gran Tarajal

****Casa Atlántica, Playa del Matorral, tel. 87 60 17, 80 r.,   Jandía Playa/Morro del
SP   Jable
***Robinson Club Jandía Playa, tel. 87 60 25, 325 r., SP
**Fiesta Casa Atlántica, Playa de Matorral, tel. 87 60 17,
116 r., SP

***Las Gabias, Avenida Marítima 3, tel. 85 12 00, 64 r.   Puerto del Rosario
***Parador Nacional de Fuerteventura, Playa Blanca,
tel. 85 11 50, 50 r., SP

**Ruben Tinguaro, Calle Juan XXIII 52, tel. 85 10 88, 9 r.
**Valerón, Candelaria del Castillo, tel. 85 06 18, 16 r.

Tarajalejo   ***Maxorata, tel. 87 00 50, 61 r., SP

Hotels on Lanzarote

Arrecife   ****Arrecife Gran Hotel, Avenida de la Mancomunidad, tel. 81 12 50, 150 r., SP
***Lancelot Playa, Avenida de la Mancomunidad, tel. 81 14 00, 123 r.
***Miramar, Calle Coll 2, tel. 81 04 38, 90 r.

Costa Teguise   *****Meliá Las Salinas, tel. 81 30 40, 310 r., SP

Playa Blanca   **Playa Blanca, tel. 83 00 46, 11 r.

Puerto del Carmen   ****Los Fariones, Playa Blanca, tel. 82 51 75, 237 r., SP
****San Antonio, Playa los Pocillos, tel. 82 50 50, 336 r., SP
**Playa Grande, Playa los Pocillos, tel. 82 52 27, 544 r.

Information

In the United Kingdom   Spanish National Tourist Office,
57–58 St James's Street,
London SW1A 1LD;
tel. (01) 499 0901

In the United States   Spanish National Tourist Office,
665 Fifth Avenue,
New York NY 10022;
tel. (212) 759 8822

245 North Michigan Avenue,
Chicago IL 60611;
tel. (312) 944 0215

1 Hallidie Plaza, Suite 801,
San Francisco CA 94012;
tel. (415) 346 8100

In Canada   Spanish National Tourist Office,
60 Bloor Street West,
Toronto, Ontario M4W 3B8;
tel. (416) 961 3131

On Gran Canaria   Casa del Turismo,
Parque Santa Catalina,
Las Palmas;
tel. 26 46 23
(Open Monday to Friday 9 a.m.–1.30 p.m. and 5–7 p.m.;
Saturday 9.30 a.m.–1 p.m.)

Patronato Insular de Turismo,
Calle León y Castillo 17,
Las Palmas;
tel. 36 22 22

On Fuerteventura

There is no official tourist information office; apply to:

Cabildo Insular,
Calle Rosario 7,
Puerto del Rosario;
tel. 85 11 08, 85 12 62

On Lanzarote

Oficina de Turismo,
Parque Municipal,
Arrecife;
tel. 81 18 60
(Irregular opening hours)

Language

In the larger hotels and restaurants in the eastern Canaries the staff usually speak either English or German. In the smaller and remoter places language may be a problem, and in these areas it is helpful to have even a smattering of Spanish.

Everyday expressions

Good morning!	¡Buenos días!
Good afternoon!	¡Buenas tardes!
Good evening, good night!	¡Buenas noches!
Goodbye!	¡Adios!
	¡Hasta luego!
Yes, no	Sí, no (señor, señora, etc.)
Please	Por favor
Thank you (very much)	(Muchas) gracias
Excuse me! (e.g. *for a mistake*)	¡Perdón!
Excuse me! (e.g. *when passing in front of someone*)	¡Con permiso!
Not at all! (You're welcome!)	¡De nada!
	¡No hay de qué!
Do you speak English?	¿Habla Usted inglés?
A little, not much	Un poco, no mucho
I do not understand	No entiendo
What is the Spanish for . . .?	¿Cómo se dice en español . . .?
What is the name of this church?	¿Cómo se llama esta iglesia?
The Cathedral (of St John)	La catedral (San Juan)
Where is Calle . . .?	¿Dónde está la calle . . .?
the road to . . .?	el camino para . . .?
To the right, left	A la derecha, izquierda
Straight ahead	Siempre derecho
Above, up	Arriba
Below, down	Abajo
When is it open, closed?	¿A qué horas está abierto, cerrado?
How far?	¿Qué distancia?
Today	Hoy
Yesterday	Ayer
The day before yesterday	Anteayer

Practical Information

Tomorrow	Mañana
Have you any rooms?	¿Hay habitaciones libres?
I should like . . .	Quisiera . . .
A room with private bath	Una habitación con baño
With full board	Con pensión completa
What does it cost?	¿Cuánto vale?
Everything included	Todo incluido
That is too dear	Es demasiado caro
Bill, please! (*to a waiter*)	¡Camarero, la cuenta, por favor!
Where is the lavatory?	¿Donde está el retrete?
Wake me at six	Llámeme Usted a las seis
Where is there a doctor?	¿Dónde hay un médico?
a dentist	un dentista?
a chemist?	una farmacia?
Help!	¡Socorro!
I have a pain here	Siento dolores aquí
I am suffering from . . .	Padezco de . . .
I need medicine for . . .	Necesito un medicamento contra . . .
How often must I take it?	¿Cuántas veces tengo que tomar esta medicina?

Days of the week

Sunday	Domingo	Thursday	Jueves
Monday	Lunes	Friday	Viernes
Tuesday	Martes	Saturday	Sábado
Wednesday	Miércoles		

Months

January	enero	July	julio
February	febrero	August	agosto
March	Marzo	September	septiembre
April	abril	October	octubre
May	mayo	November	noviembre
June	junio	December	diciembre

Numbers

0	cero	22	veintidós
1	uno, una	30	treinta
2	dos	31	treinta y uno
3	tres	40	cuarenta
4	cuatro	50	cincuenta
5	cinco	60	sesenta
6	seis	70	setenta
7	siete	80	ochenta
8	ocho	90	noventa
9	nueve	100	ciento (cien)
10	diez	101	ciento uno
11	once	153	ciento cincuenta y tres
12	doce	200	doscientos
13	trece	300	trescientos
14	catorce	400	cuatrocientos
15	quince	500	quinientos
16	dieciséis	600	seiscientos
17	diecisiete	700	setecientos
18	dieciocho	800	ochocientos
19	diecinueve	900	novecientos
20	veinte	1000	mil
21	veintiuno	1,000,000	un millón

Geographical, etc., terms

Acantilado	Rocky coast
Ayuntamiento	Town hall
Bahía	Bay
Barranco	Gorge
Barrio	District, quarter (of a town)
Bosque	Wood, forest
Calle	Street
Camino	Road, track, path
Capilla	Chapel
Carretera	(Main) road
Cementerio	Cemetery, churchyard
Ciudad	City, town
Claustro	Cloister
Convento	Monastery, convent
Costa	Coast
Cuesta	Slope, hill
Cueva	Cave
Cumbre	Summit
Ermita	Chapel, small church
Faro	Lighthouse
Fuente	Fountain, spring
Iglesia	Church
Jardín	Garden
Llano	Plain
Mar	Sea
Mirador	Viewpoint
Montaña, monte	Mountain, hill
Paisaje	Landscape
Parque	Park
Paseo	Avenue, promenade
Patio	Courtyard
Peña	Crag, cliff
Pico	Peak, summit
Playa	Beach
Plaza	Square
Pueblo	Village
Puente	Bridge
Puerta	Door(way)
Puerto	Port, harbour; pass
Punta	Point, headland
Río	River
Roque	Rock
Sierra	Mountain range
Torre	Tower
Torrente	Mountain stream
Urbanización	Housing development
Valle	Valley

Leisure parks

Go-Kart Racing   On Gran Canaria
Situation: 2 km (1¼ miles) north-west of Maspalomas on
the El Tablero road.
A variety of karts (junior, special, racing, double) can be
hired. As a special attraction for children there are also

motor-driven "bumper boats". Spectator terrace with restaurant. Open daily 10 a.m.–11 p.m.
Holiday World

See A to Z, Playa del Inglés/Maspalomas

Jardín Canario
See A to Z, Tafira

Palmitos Parque
See A to Z, Playa del Inglés/Maspalomas

Sioux City
See A to Z, San Agustín

Marinas

Gran Canaria

Real Club Náutico de Gran Canaria,
Puerto de la Luz, Las Palmas;
tel. 24 66 90

Puerto Deportivo,
Puerto de Mogán;
tel. 74 02 22

El Castillo marina, Fuerteventura

Puerto Deportivo de Club de Yates,
Pasito Blanco (3 km/2 miles west of Maspalomas);
tel. 76 22 59

Puerto Deportivo,
Puerto Rico;
tel. 74 57 57

There are marinas at Corralejo, Morro del Jable and El Castillo.

Fuerteventura

There are marinas at Arrecife and Playa Blanca and on the Costa Teguise.

Lanzarote

Medical care

There are adequate medical services on all the islands. Most of the doctors speak at least one foreign language. In case of emergency apply to one of the hospitals listed below or to a casualty station (see Emergency calls).

British citizens, like nationals of other EEC countries, are entitled to obtain medical care under the Spanish health services on the same basis as Spanish people. This means that they can get free medical and hospital treatment but will be required to pay charges for prescribed medicines or dental treatment.

Health insurance

Before leaving home they should ask their local social security office for a booklet entitled "Medical costs abroad" (SA 30), which contains an application for form E 111. This is the document which entitles them to treatment from a "National Health" (INSALUD) doctor. The addresses of doctors can be obtained from INSALUD or from the Instituto Nacional de la Seguridad Social.

It is nevertheless advisable, even for EEC nationals, to take out some form of short-term health insurance providing complete cover and possibly avoiding bureaucratic delays; and nationals of non-EEC countries should certainly have insurance cover.

On Gran Canaria:
Calle Leon y Castillo 224, Las Palmas,
tel. 23 32 99

INSALUD

On Gran Canaria:
Avenida Juan XXIII 11, Las Palmas, tel. 23 45 15
There are also offices in Arucas, Gáldar, Telde and Vecindario (Sardina del Sur).

Instituto Nacional de la
Seguridad Social

On Fuerteventura:
Calle Almirante Lallemand, Puerto del Rosario, tel. 85 02 70

On Lanzarote:
Calle Fajardo 21, Arrecife, tel. 81 11 02

Practical Information

Hospitals	Clínica Internacional, Calle Núñez de Arce 2, Las Palmas, Gran Canaria; tel. 24 56 43
	Hospital Insular, Plaza Doctor Pasteur, Las Palmas, Gran Canaria; tel. 31 30 33
	Clínica San Agustín, Calle Buganvillas 1, San Agustín, Gran Canaria; tel. 76 27 03
	Hospital Insular, Calle Juan de Quesada, Arrecife, Lanzarote; tel. 81 05 00
	Hospital Seguridad Social, Carretera General al Aeropuerto, Puerto del Rosario, Fuerteventura; tel. 85 10 59
Dental clinics	Clínica Dental, Calle Perdomo 45, Las Palmas, Gran Canaria; tel. 36 33 08
	Clínica Dental, Avenida de Tirajana, San Agustín, Gran Canaria; tel. 76 32 80
Emergency calls	See entry

Motoring

In the Canaries, as in mainland Spain and the rest of continental Europe, traffic travels on the right, with overtaking (passing) on the left.

Speed limits

120 km p.h. (74½ m.p.h.) on motorways.
100 km p.h. (62 m.p.h.) on roads with two or more lanes in each direction.
90 km p.h. (56 m.p.h.) on other roads.
60 km p.h. (37 m.p.h.) in built-up areas.

Seat belts

Seat belts must be worn outside built-up areas.

Lights

On well-lighted streets and roads (except expressways and motorways) driving with sidelights is permitted. A careful lookout should be kept for vehicles driving without lights.

Priority

In general, traffic coming from the right has priority, and this applies also on roundabouts. Exceptions to the rule are indicated by signs.

154

When overtaking (passing) the left-hand indicator light must be kept on during the whole process and the right-hand one operated when pulling in to the right. Drivers about to overtake, or approaching a bend, must sound their horn during the day and flash their lights at night.
Overtaking is prohibited within 100 m (110 yd) of a blind summit and on roads with a visibility of less than 200 m (220 yd).

Overtaking

The blood alcohol limit is 0.8 per 1000.

Blood alcohol limit

Visitors travelling in a rented car should contact the office of the firm from which they hired it.
If you have a breakdown in your own car help can be obtained from the Policia Municipal (see Police) in towns and from the Guardia Civil de Tráfico in the country.

Breakdown assistance

An accident can have very serious consequences for a foreign driver. Whether the accident is his fault or not, his car may be impounded (and may be released only after the completion of any judicial proceedings that follow), and in serious cases the driver may be arrested.
After any accident the Spanish insurance company named on the driver's "green card" must be informed without delay, so that arrangements may be made for any payment required in the way of bail.
The towing of a broken-down vehicle by a private car is prohibited.
In the event of an accident involving a hired car the instructions in the hire documents should be followed.

Accidents

Real Automóvil Club de Gran Canaria,
Calle León y Castillo 57,
Las Palmas;
tel. 36 61 88

Automobile clubs

Touring Club de España,
Calle León y Castillo 279,
Las Palmas;
tel. 23 01 88
Manned 24 hours a day; breakdown service

Museums

Casa de Colón
See A to Z, Las Palmas

Gran Canaria

Casa de los Patronos de la Virgen del Pino
See A to Z, Teror

Museo Canario
See A to Z, Las Palmas

Museo Néstor
See A to Z, Las Palmas

Museo de Pérez Galdós
See A to Z, Las Palmas

	Museo de Piedras y Artesanía Canaria See A to Z, Ingenio
	Museo Diocesano de Arte Sacro See A to Z, Las Palmas
	Museo León y Castillo See A to Z, Telde
Fuerteventura	Museo Arqueológico See A to Z, Fuerteventura: Betancuria
Lanzarote	Museo Arqueológico See A to Z, Lanzarote: Arrecife (Castillo de San Gabriel)
	Museo Internacional de Arte Contemporáneo See A to Z, Lanzarote: Arrecife (Castillo de San José)
	Palacio de Spínola See A to Z, Lanzarote: Teguise

Newspapers and periodicals

Major British newspapers and periodicals are on sale on Gran Canaria the day after publication, as is the "International Herald Tribune". On the other islands it may take longer, and the choice will be more restricted.

The English-language "Island Gazette", published monthly, gives local news and information about excursions, restaurants, etc. Other useful English-language publications are the bi-monthly "Canarias Tourist" and the quarterly "Holiday Times".

Night life

Casino	Casino Gran Canaria, Hotel Tamarindos, San Agustín (French and American roulette, baccarat, blackjack, etc.) Open daily 9 p.m. to 4 a.m. (Consideration is being given to the granting of further licences)
Discos, night clubs	There are large numbers of discothèques and night clubs in the tourist centres on Gran Canaria, particularly Playa del Inglés/Maspalomas. There are occasional flamenco shows in the Aladinos night club in Playa del Inglés. On Fuerteventura and Lanzarote there are night clubs and discothèques in the large hotels.

Opening times

Banks	Monday to Friday 9 a.m.–2 p.m., Saturday 9 a.m.–1 p.m.
Chemists	Monday to Friday 9 a.m.–1 p.m. and 4–8 p.m., Saturday 9 a.m.–1 p.m.

Churches are usually open in the morning and late after-noon as well as for services.

Churches

The opening times of museums vary: see the entries in the A to Z section.

Museums

Monday to Friday 9 a.m.–1 p.m. and 3–7 p.m., Saturday 9 a.m.–1 p.m.

Offices

Most petrol stations close at 8 or 10 p.m., but some on Gran Canaria are open 24 hours a day. On Sunday all petrol stations on Fuerteventura and Lanzarote and almost all stations on Gran Canaria are closed.

Petrol stations

Monday to Friday 9 a.m.–2 p.m., Saturday 9 a.m.–1 p.m.

Post offices

Restaurants usually close about midnight or 1 a.m.

Restaurants

Most shops are open Monday to Friday 9 a.m.–1 p.m. and 4–8 p.m., Saturday 9 a.m.–1 p.m.; but there are no fixed closing times in Spain, and supermarkets and other shops, particularly in the tourist centres, are often open outside these hours and sometimes on Sundays as well.

Shops

Police

See Emergency calls

Policia Municipal
(town and traffic police)

Gran Canaria:
Calle Canalejas 86, Las Palmas;
tel. 37 03 44
Carretera General del Sur, San Agustín;
tel. 76 39 71

Policia Nacional
(tourist police, criminal police)

Lanzarote:
Calle Coll 5, Arrecife;
tel. 81 36 36

Gran Canaria:
Calle Millares 16, Las Palmas;
tel. 32 04 00
Urbanización San Fernando de Maspalomas, San Agustín;
tel. 76 28 98

Guardia Civil
(country police, criminal police)

Fuerteventura:
Calle Veintitrés de Mayo 16, Puerto del Rosario;
tel. 85 11 00

Lanzarote:
Calle El Júpiter, Arrecife;
tel. 81 09 46

Postal and telephone services

All letters and postcards from the Canaries go by air. Mail, takes at least five days to reach northern Europe.

Postal service

Practical Information

	Postage (to Europe):	
	letters up to 20 grams	45 ptas
	(non-EEC countries)	50 ptas
	postcards	45 ptas

Post-boxes   Spanish post-boxes (pillar-boxes) are yellow.

Post offices   Post and telegraph offices (Correos y Telégrafos) are open Monday to Friday 9 a.m.–2 p.m., Saturday 9 a.m.–1 p.m. Telephone calls cannot be made from post offices.

Telegrams   Telegrams can be sent from post offices or dictated by telephone (dial 22 20 00).

Telephoning   No dialling code is required for calls within the province of Las Palmas de Gran Canaria (which includes the islands of Fuerteventura and Lanzarote).
International calls can be made from coin-operated public telephones bearing the word *internacional*. These take 5, 25, 50 and 100 peseta coins. To make a call, first dial 07; then, when the high-pitched dialling tone is heard, dial the appropriate international code (44 for the United Kingdom, 1 for the United States or Canada), followed by the local dialling code (omitting an initial zero) and the subscriber's number. A faint dialling tone is heard during dialling. For a call of some length it is preferable to go to one of the public telephone offices (only in the larger towns, and open only at certain times), where payment is made on termination of the call.

Directory enquiries   Local (within the province of Las Palmas de Gran Canaria): 003
International: 91 98

Dialling codes   From the United Kingdom to the eastern Canaries (province of Las Palmas de Gran Canaria): 010 34 28

From the United States or Canada to the province of Las Palmas de Gran Canaria: 011 34 28

From within Spain to the province of Las Palmas de Gran Canaria: 9 28

From within Spain to the province of Santa Cruz de Tenerife: 9 22

From the Canaries to the United Kingdom: 07 44

From the Canaries to the United States or Canada: 07 1

Public holidays

Fixed feasts

1 January	Año Nuevo (New Year's Day)
6 January	Los Reyes (Epiphany)
19 March	San José (St Joseph's Day)
1 May	Día del Trabajo (Labour Day)
30 May	Dia de las Canarias (Day of the Canaries)
25 July	Santiago (St James's Day)
15 August	Asunción (Assumption)
12 October	Día de la Hispanidad (discovery of America)

1 November	Todos los Santos (All Saints)
6 December	Día de la Constitucion (Constitution Day)
8 December	Inmaculada Concepción (Immaculate Conception)
25 December	Navidad (Christmas Day)

Jueves Santo (Maundy Thursday)   Movable feasts
Viernes Santo (Good Friday)
Corpus Christi

See Events   Local feasts

Radio and television

Most television programmes in the Canaries are relayed
from the mainland and are in Spanish. On short wave radio
the BBC World Service and the Voice of America can be
heard clearly at night and in the early morning. Brief news
and music programmes in English are broadcast mornings
and evenings from Las Palmas and twice daily from Tenerife.

Restaurants

In the tourist areas on Gran Canaria, Fuerteventura and
Lanzarote there are large numbers of restaurants in every
category. If, however, you want something more than the
kind of standard international menu that so many of them
offer you may have to look around a little.

Restaurants on Gran Canaria

*Puerto Atlántico, tel. 73 53 41   Arguineguín

La Farola, Calle Alcalá Faliano 3, tel. 75 26 84   Arinaga

Mesón de la Montaña, Montaña de Arucas, tel. 60 14 75   Arucas

Hostería Nacional. tel. 65 80 50   Cruz de Tejeda

*Acuario, Plaza de España 3, tel. 27 34 32   Las Palmas
Canario, Calle Perojo 2, tel. 36 57 16
El Herreño, Calle Mendizábal 5–7, tel. 31 05 13
El Pote, Pasaje José María Durán 11, tel. 27 80 58
Julio, Calle La Naval 132, tel. 27 10 39
La Cabana Criolla, Calle Los Martínez de Escobar 37,
tel. 27 02 16
Mesón La Paella, Pasaje José María Durán 47, tel. 27 16 40
Pitango, Calle María Dolorosa 2, tel. 26 38 94
Samoa, Calle Valencia 46, tel. 24 14 71

*El Tenderete, Avenida de Tirajana, tel. 76 14 60   Playa del Inglés/
*Orangerie, Palm Beach Hotel, tel. 76 29 20   Maspalomas
La Toja, Avenida de Tirajana, tel. 76 11 96
Mesón El Gallego, Avenida Gran Canaria 33, tel. 76 11 45

Practical Information

Puerto de las Nieves	Antonio, tel. 89 81 71
Puerto Rico	Puerto Rico, Paseo de la Playa, tel. 74 51 81
San Agustín	*San Agustín Beach Club, Plaza de los Cocoteros 1, tel. 76 03 70 Buganvilla, Calle Morro Besudo 17, tel. 76 03 16 Chez Mario, Calle Los Pinos 15, Urbanización Nueva Europa, tel. 76 18 17
Santa Brígida	Bentayga, Carretera de las Palmas, tel. 35 02 45 El Palmeral, Avenida del Palmeral 45, tel. 64 15 18 Las Grutas de Artiles, Las Meleguinas, tel. 64 05 75
Tafira Alta	Jardín Canario, Plan de Loreto, Carretera de las Palmas, tel. 35 16 45
Teror	San Matías, Carretera de Arucas, tel. 63 07 65

Restaurants on Fuerteventura

Corralejo	Oscar, Calle de la Iglesia 9, tel. 86 61 96
Lajita	Cuesta de la Pared, Urbanización Puerto Rico
Morro del Jable	Laja, Puerto

Restaurants on Lanzarote

Arrecife	*Picasso, Calle José Betancort 33, tel. 81 24 16 Abdon, Calle Canalejas 54, tel. 81 45 58 Castillo de San José, tel. 81 23 21 Martín, Plaza de la Constitución 12, tel. 81 23 54
Costa Teguise	La Chimenea, Playa de las Cucharas, tel. 81 47 00 Tabaiba, Playa de las Cucharas, tel. 81 17 07
Montañas del Fuego	Del Diablo, tel. 84 00 57
Playa Blanca	Playa, Las Puntas, tel. 82 52 76
Puerto del Carmen	*Dionysios, Centro Comercial Roque Nublo, tel. 82 52 55 La Bohème, Avenida de las Playas 51, Club Villas Blancas, tel. 82 59 15 La Gaviota, Centro Marina Bay, tel. 82 50 50 Romántica II, Centro Atlántico, tel. 82 57 20
Yaiza	La Era, tel. 83 00 16
Complaints	Restaurants, like hotels, are required to keep a "complaints book" (*libro de reclamaciones*), which is inspected by the authorities. Complaints by dissatisfied clients should be entered in this book, giving name and home address; entries may be made in English.

Shopping

Since 1852 the Canaries have been a free trade (duty-free) zone. This does not necessarily mean that all prices are low, for shops do not always pass on the benefit of the tax exemption to the customer.
Tobacco goods will be found to be considerably cheaper than at home, and the prices of spirits and perfumes are also relatively low. Cameras and other technical equipment, and also furs, can sometimes be found at prices that appear very reasonable; but purchases should be made only in specialised shops and after a careful check on quality.

Free trade zone

The best shopping streets in Las Palmas are Calle Triana and Avenida Mesa y López.

Shopping streets

The markets held in many small towns and villages in the country (for example Teror or Vega de San Mateo), usually on Sundays, are full of interest for visitors. At San Fernando (near Maspalomas) and Arguineguín the market is held on Tuesday morning. In addition to fruit, vegetables, cheese and peasant bread the goods on offer sometimes include local craft products.

Markets

A great variety of local hand-crafted articles are offered for sale on the islands. A typical Canarian product is the small stringed instrument known as a *timple.* The best embroidery comes from Ingenio (Gran Canaria). The attractive local pottery is still sometimes produced in the traditional way without the use of a wheel. Basketwork, using palm fronds, reeds or osiers, is found all over the islands. Seeds and seedlings of indigenous plants, or a bunch of strelitzias (sold in flower shops ready packed for the flight home) will provide an attractive reminder of the flora of the Canaries. For those who want to take back an alcoholic souvenir of their visit there is Spanish brandy – among the best brands are Lepanto, Duque de Alba and Carlos I – and the banana liqueur of the Canaries.

Souvenirs

Sport

The Canaries are a paradise for deep-sea anglers, with good fishing grounds only 2 miles off the coasts.

Deep-sea angling

The coastal waters of the Canaries offer ideal conditions for scuba diving and snorkelling. Many hotels run courses for beginners and more experienced divers. The marine flora and fauna are particularly interesting in the Underwater Park at Arinaga on Gran Canaria (two diving schools), off the north coast of Fuerteventura at Corralejo and at Morro del Jable in the south of the island.

Diving

Campo de Golf de Bandama,
Los Toscones (15 km/9 miles SW of Las Palmas), Gran Canaria
18 holes; length 5.7 km/6200 yd
Tel. 35 10 50

Golf

Golf on the Campo de Bandama

Wind-surfers on Fuerteventura

Campo de Maspalomas, Maspalomas, Gran Canaria
16 holes; length 3.2 km/3500 yds
Tel. 76 25 81

Campo de Golf,
Costa Teguise (at Las Salinas Sheraton Hotel), Lanzarote
27 holes

Minigolf

San Valentín Park,
Calle Timple, Playa del Inglés, Gran Canaria
Daily 9 a.m.–11 p.m.

There are other minigolf courses on Gran Canaria at San Agustín and Puerto Rico.

Riding

Horses can be hired at the Rancho Park (near the Palmitos Park at Maspalomas, Gran Canaria), which also gives riding instruction and organises pony treks.
There are other riding schools on Gran Canaria at the Bandama golf club and on the road between Marzagán and Tafira.

Sailing, wind-surfing

On some stretches of coast there are fairly strong winds, making these areas unsuitable for beginners.
The south and south-west coasts of Gran Canaria offer ideal conditions for sailing and wind-surfing. Sailing courses are organised at Puerto Rico. Surf-boards can be hired at Playa del Inglés, San Agustín, Puerto de Mogán and Puerto Rico.

Pozo Izquierdo, at El Doctoral, is favoured by experienced
wind-surfers.
On Fuerteventura the beaches of Corralejo, Morro del Jable
and Playa de Cotillo are good surfing areas. For beginners
there is a wind-surfing school at El Castillo.
On Lanzarote the Playa de los Pocillos, Playa de Famara and
Playa de Fariones offer excellent surfing.

The shooting season for small game (partridges, pigeons,   Shooting (hunting)
rabbits) is from the first Sunday in August to the last Sun-
day in December. Information: Sociedad de Cazadores,
Calle Venegas 11, Las Palmas, tel. 36 33 09.

Many of the large hotels on Gran Canaria, Fuerteventura   Tennis
and Lanzarote have excellent tennis courts, sometimes
equipped with floodlighting. Coaching is usually available.
Some hotels (e.g. the Helga Masthoff hotel at Palmitos
Park, Maspalomas, Gran Canaria) offer all-in tennis holiday
packages.

See entry   Walking

There are facilities for water-skiing on Gran Canaria at Playa   Water-skiing
del Inglés, the "Aquamarina" (between Arguineguín and
Puerto Rico) and Puerto Rico.

Of particular interest to visitors are the traditional local   Canarian sports
sports, the best known of which is Canarian wrestling
(*lucha canaria*). In almost every place of any size there is a
ring on which contests are held between twelve-man teams
of wrestlers.

The *juego de palo*, a contest like singlesticks, with two sticks
instead of one, is also fascinating to watch. Each contestant
has to attack his opponent and ward off his blows while
moving his body as little as possible.

Another Canarian diversion is cock-fighting, which is the
subject of heavy betting. During the season (December to
May) there are cock-fights in the López Socas Stadium in
Las Palmas on Sundays and public holidays.

There is a bullring at Maspalomas on Gran Canaria in which   Bullfighting
bullfights are held at irregular intervals.

Taxis

Most taxis have meters; for journeys of some length, however, there are usually fixed rates. The rate per kilometre is
about 60 pesetas (one-way; if the same taxi is used for the
return journey it is much cheaper). Waiting time is charged
extra. To avoid any misunderstanding it is advisable to ask
about the fare before setting out: taxi-drivers are required
to carry the official tariff and to produce it if necessary.

Telegraph and telephone services

See Postal and telephone services

Theft

Theft is unfortunately a common occurrence in the large tourist centres. It is advisable, therefore, to keep objects of value and personal papers in the safes provided in many hotel rooms or to hand them to the hotel management for safe keeping. Never leave anything in a hired car, for, particularly in Las Palmas, it is liable to be broken into at any time of the day or night. Even when driving it is wise to keep the car doors and the boot locked: there are youths, again particularly in Las Palmas, whose speciality is, when cars are stopped at traffic lights, to offer to wash the windscreen, and who have then a good opportunity to steal something from the car.

Time

The Canaries observe Greenwich Mean Time (Western European Time), one hour earlier than the time in mainland Spain and five hours later than Eastern Standard Time in the United States. From April to September Summer Time is in force, the same as British Summer Time and five hours later than Eastern Daylight Saving Time.

As a result of the islands' nearness to the Equator the evenings are relatively long in winter (with sunset about 7 p.m.) and short in summer.

Tipping

In general a service charge is included in bills, but hotel staff, waiters, taxi-drivers, etc., expect an additional tip of 5–10 per cent of the bill.

Transport

Buses

The larger towns and villages on Gran Canaria are connected by a network of bus services. The different parts of the island are most easily reached from Las Palmas; the main bus station is in the Avenida Rafael Cabrera, at the Parque San Telmo. There are buses every half-hour to Puerto Rico (last departure about 9.30 p.m.) and roughly every two hours to Mogán (last departure about 7.30 p.m.), and a direct service to Maspalomas and Playa del Inglés every 20 minutes (last departure about 7.30 p.m.).

Most places on Fuerteventura and Lanzarote are on a bus route, but buses tend to be few and far between. As a general rule buses leave outlying places for the capital early in the morning, with a return service in the afternoon.

On Lanzarote there are better services between Puerto del Carmen and Arrecife, with buses roughly every hour. Between Playa Blanca and Arrecife there are three buses a day.

See entry	Car rental
See entry	Taxis
See entry	Air services
	Boat services

All the islands are connected by regular services run by the Compañía Trasmediterránea (see plan on inside back cover). Information can be obtained from the Compañía Trasmediterránea (see Getting to the eastern Canaries).

There are three sailings weekly between Las Palmas (Gran Canaria) and Puerto del Rosario (Fuerteventura). There is a daily ferry between Las Palmas and Santa Cruz (Tenerife). A jetfoil runs from Mon. to Thur. and on Sat., from Santa Cruz via Las Palmas to Morro Jable (Fuerteventura).

The Compañía Trasmediterránea runs a twice-weekly service between Arrecife and Puerto del Rosario. Much more convenient, however, is the service by ship between Corralejo (Fuerteventura) and Playa Blanca (Lanzarote: crossing time about 40 min., or 20 by jetfoil). The Betancuria ferry

Jetfoil at full speed

does this crossing three times a day, and the Alisur ship four times. In addition, a jetfoil goes daily from Puerto del Rosario via Corralejo and Playa Blanca and back to Puerto del Rosario.

There are services from Fuerteventura (Corralejo) to Lobos and from Lanzarote (El Embarcadero) to Graciosa in converted fishing boats, which do not sail in bad weather.

Travel documents

Personal papers

Visitors from the United Kingdom, the Commonwealth and the United States must have a valid passport. No visa is required by nationals of the United Kingdom, Australia, Canada and New Zealand for a stay of up to three months, or by United States nationals for a stay of up to six months, provided in each case that they are not taking up any paid employment. An extension of stay can be granted by the police authorities.

Car papers

A national driving licence is acceptable in Spain, but must be accompanied by an official translation stamped by a Spanish consulate; it may be easier and cheaper to carry an international driving permit (which is required in any event for business trips).

The car registration document must be carried, and the car must bear an oval nationality plate.

An international insurance certificate (green card) is required, and also a bail bond (issued by an insurance company with the green card), since in the event of an accident the car may be impounded pending payment of bail (see Motoring).

N.B.

It is advisable to make photocopies of your travel documents and take them with you. This makes it easier to get replacements if you lose the originals.

Walking

Although the eastern Canaries are less suited for a walking holiday than Tenerife, Gomera, Hierro and La Palma, there are good walks to be had, particularly on Gran Canaria. The interior of the island is particularly good walking country, with its varied scenery, luxuriant vegetation and excellent climate. A very useful and attractive guide to walks on Gran Canaria is Noel Rochford's "Landscapes of Gran Canaria" (Sunflower Books, London, 1986).

Long walks should be undertaken only with proper equipment. The going is sometimes rough and stony, requiring stout footwear, preferably boots. For protection against the strong sun a hat and sun cream are essential. In view of possible changes in the weather some protection against rain should be taken, and in winter warm clothing is necessary.

When to go

The Canaries are sometimes called the "islands of eternal spring" – a reputation they owe to a climate which remains equable throughout the year (see Facts and Figures, Climate). The temperature variation between the warmest and the coldest month is barely 6 °C (11 °F), and bathing is possible all year round. During the winter months, therefore, the islands attract large numbers of visitors from sun-starved Central and Northern Europe.

From the point of view of vegetation a good time to visit the Canaries is March, when the flora of the islands is seen in all its splendour.

While in winter accommodation in the Canaries must be booked well in advance, during the summer many hotels are almost empty. However Gran Canaria, Fuerteventura and Lanzarote are also very agreeable at this time of year, when oppressively hot and sultry days are rare.

Weather table	Temperature in °C (°F)				Sun-shine (hours per day)	Rainy days	Rain-fall in mm (in)
	Air						
Months	Max.	Min.	Mean	Sea			
January	22.5 (72.5)	15.0 (59.0)	19.5 (67.1)	19.0 (66.2)	6.1	9	36.65 (1.44)
February	23.0 (73.4)	15.0 (59.0)	19.5 (67.1)	19.3 (66.7)	8.9	2	8.25 (0.32)
March	26.0 (78.8)	14.7 (58.5)	18.6 (65.5)	18.7 (65.7)	7.7	2	1.80 (0.07)
April	22.3 (72.1)	16.2 (61.2)	19.6 (67.3)	19.0 (66.2)	7.7	6	11.55 (0.45)
May	24.7 (76.5)	17.5 (63.5)	20.6 (69.1)	19.7 (67.5)	8.7	2	1.85 (0.07)
June	25.8 (78.4)	18.2 (64.8)	21.2 (70.2)	20.9 (69.6)	10.3	0	–
July	25.8 (78.4)	20.0 (68.0)	23.5 (74.3)	22.2 (72.0)	9.8	0	–
August	28.5 (83.3)	20.5 (68.9)	24.2 (75.6)	22.3 (72.0)	8.3	0	–
September	26.0 (76.8)	19.5 (67.1)	24.0 (75.2)	23.3 (73.9)	6.0	3	6.20 (0.24)
October	25.7 (78.3)	20.2 (68.4)	23.0 (73.4)	22.3 (72.0)	5.9	2	3.70 (0.15)
November	23.8 (74.8)	18.1 (64.6)	20.9 (69.6)	23.1 (73.6)	5.6	9	58.20 (2.29)
December	22.7 (72.9)	15.5 (59.9)	19.0 (66.2)	20.2 (68.4)	5.0	4	9.60 (0.38)
Year	24.7 (76.5)	17.5 (63.5)	21.3 (70.3)	20.8 (69.4)	7.5	39	137.80 (5.43)

Youth Hostels

"San Fernando" Youth Hostel, Avenida Juventud, Santa Maria de Guia (Gran Canaria), tel. 88 27 28

Index

(F = Fuerteventura; G = Gran Canaria; L = Lanzarote)

Index

Notes

Notes